SONGAIA

An Unfolding Dream

The Story of a Community's
Journey into Being

SONGAIA

An Unfolding Dream

The Story of a Community's Journey into Being

Fred Lanphear

With Contributions from
Songaia Community Members

SONGAIA

An Unfolding Dream

The Story of a Community's Journey into Being

Published by

Songaia Press

2401 224th St. SE

Bothell, WA 98021

(425) 481-8044

www.songaia.com

Cover and interior design by
Robert Lanphear / Lanphear Design
www.lanpheardesign.com

Lanphear, Fred.
Songaia: an unfolding dream, the story of a community's
journey into being / Fred Lanphear

ISBN: 978-0615579788

I dedicate this book to my beautiful wife Nancy, who shared with me the belief that to give your life to something you believe in is one of the greatest expressions of love. Thank you for sharing your life with me. Your love, support and commitment made this all possible. Carry on, continue your work and know that you are loved.

*My great work is where my own greatest joy
intersects with Earth's great need.*

—Thomas Berry

Contents

Acknowledgments

Much gratitude to the many community members that shared in our experiences and perspectives. Families residing at Songaia as this book was being written (in alphabetical order): Kate Arden; Barb and Brian Bansenauer, with their son Ian; Kevin Benedict with his son Cory; Carol and Stan Crow; Dorothy Fulton and Brent Stuart; Susie Fox; Michelle Grandy and Tom Barr, with their daughter Amelia; Marilyn and Chuck Hanna-Myrick; Cyndi and Tad Kershner, with their son Lucas; Nancy Lanphear; Douglas Larson, with his daughter Risa Lisette; Jean Mohr; Karly Lubach and Craig Ragland; Danielle and James Olson, with their children Alaina, Christopher, and Alexander; Scott Buckley, Patrick Paul and Marlin Wilson; Selima; Kathleen Stern and Larry Magnoni; Sadhana Fricke and Nartano Scharnhorst, with their children Natasha, Suzanne, and Lilly; Rachel Lynnette, with her children David and Lucy; Katie and Michael Stein, with their children Aviana and Kaiden; and Helen Gabel and Phil Noterman.

A generous acknowledgment to all who helped in the production of the book including assisting Fred with typing: Lucas Kershner, editing/proofreading: Robyn Fritz, Rachel Lynnette, Robert Lanphear, Craig Ragland and Chris Wade; transcription: Cheryl Green; childrens' interviews: Leah Early; project management: Brian Bansenauer, Robert Lanphear, Nancy Lanphear, Michelle Grandy and Craig Ragland; and layout and design: Robert Lanphear.

As we publish this book, Fred has left us but the community carries on excited about the future and fortunate for the gift of *Songaia: An Unfolding Dream*. This book was always intended for the enjoyment of community members, friends and colleagues, but it was also meant as a way to share with the world and future generations the story of Songaia and the seeds of community: share it, gift it, use it and go to **www.songaia.com/books** to order copies.

Preface

The seeds of this book were planted over twenty years ago when a small group of people living together on a fertile 11-acre farm in western Washington decided they wanted to give form to the their dream of community. Many of them had experience in communal living and consensus building and a common vision soon crystallized among the group. Modeling their neighborhood on a european concept called cohousing, they began the process of defining their values and creating their comunity. The roots of what was to become Songaia Community took hold in anticipation of an exciting new growth and two decades of extraordinary unfolding that this book attempts to capture.

Fast forward to 2007, Songaia is in full bloom, the original vision of cohousing has been realized, the community is thriving and the neighborhood is expanding. Fred Lanphear, a founding member, initiated Earth Elder and author of this book learned that he had ALS, a degenerative and terminal diagnosis, and had maybe 3-5 years to live. In familiar fashion, Fred turned this challenge inside out, creating an opportunity to write the story of his community, something very dear to him. For as much as he was a gardener at heart, a son of the soil and passionate about cultivating community and cooperation, he was also a teacher and, whether in words or deeds, sharing his experience was all part of the cycle of life.

For the next three years, with help and contributions from many of the members of the community, he pulled together and edited these words, up until and including his final weeks alive. For him it was a labor of love, as it culminated his forty plus years experience as a builder of community. Nonetheless, in his eyes, he *facilitated* the creation of this book—it was never about him—it was always a community project, and he couldn't have done it without the assistance and input from so many people.

CHAPTER ONE

Introduction

The stories and vignettes contained in this book capture the experiences of life at Songaia, a cohousing community in Bothell, Washington. The goal is to provide a glimpse into the birth and "unfolding" of the community, focusing on events that helped Songaians themselves understand what life in community is about. *Songaia: An Unfolding Dream* describes one community's story of their evolving journey, a story that required changes and additions to the text, reflecting ongoing life in the community, right up through the proofing phase of this book.

This is not a book on how to build community. While there is material here that will inform that question, this is a story about a community and its journey—how it came to be and what it's like to live in that community. It is a community autobiography.

I've learned from experience that what people expect community to be like will always be quite different than what they actually find. This is revealed in some of the individual stories of Songaia community members. It is my hope that, in the context of any pre-conceived ideas of community, whether idyllic or cynical, the reader will gain a clearer picture of authentic community living.

In interviews with community members I often encountered abstract reasoning and theory. However, I was not looking for what they think community is about; instead, I wanted personal stories of how they actually experienced community at Songaia. One thing that shows up in these stories is how each of us brings our own passions, our own inner yearnings to a community setting. When we intertwine our lives by living together, we're given an opportunity to channel our passions in a way that benefits the whole community.

My role in writing this book has not been to focus on my experiences; instead I have taken authentic experiences of others and linked them together with a narrative. Aside from the role of narrator, my other contributions have been editorial. I have put rambling conversations into story form, condensed long stories to short ones, and discarded irrelevant trains of thought (even though some were fascinating).

A Description of Songaia

Songaia has 13 residential units located on a 11-acre plot with a gentle west facing slope. At the top of the slope is four acres of second growth Douglas fir interspersed with alder and western red cedar. The bottom of the slope is approximately three acres of grassy meadow, garden and fruit trees. The midsection contains the residential units, common house, and a two-story multipurpose barn. The access road and parking are on the northern boundary and peripheral to the residential area. The common house is adjacent to the access road and the residential units are duplexes that form a circle around the Commons. An asphalt walkway links the common house and residential units.

Songaia is located in the suburbs 15 miles northeast of Seattle. The nearest shopping center is about 3 miles away. Public transit is within 0.5 miles. The community is largely dependent on cars as a primary mode of travel. Some members occasionally use bicycles.

Two of the units have daylight-basement rental space. When the residential units and rental spaces are fully occupied we have 15 families living at Songaia. The number of individuals has varied between 31 and 38. The turnover rate of residential units has been relatively low, with only two families moving out of the community during the first 10 years. It has been higher for the rental space.

The name Songaia was created by combining the word "song" with "Gaia," the Greek mythological representation of the living Earth. These two words capture our love for singing and our value of living lightly on the earth. Songaia, or song of the living Earth, has been a unifying symbol for the community.

An Intentional Community

An Intentional Community is a group of people who choose to live together for mutual socialization and support. They come together around a common vision and shared values. The intent is to live co-operatively, making decisions collectively, and sharing resources and life experiences.

Some of the earliest forms of intentional communities were formed around religious values. Such communities continue to exist. During the 19th century a variety of communities striving for social ideals dotted the American landscape. These are sometimes referred to as utopian communities. In the 1970s there was a brief resurgence of communal living, negatively referred to as "hippie communes." These were mostly short lived. A recent resurgence has occurred around a form of community known as cohousing.

Songaia is a cohousing community. The concept of cohousing was introduced to the United States from Denmark in 1988. The characteristics that define cohousing, according to the Cohousing Association of America, are as follows:

1. Participatory process: Future residents participate in the design of the community so that it meets their needs.
2. Neighborhood design: The physical layout and orientation of the buildings (the site plan) encourage a sense of community.

3. Common facilities: Common facilities are designed for daily use, are an integral part of the community, and are always supplemental to the private residences.

4. Resident management: Residents manage their own cohousing communities, and also perform much of the work required to maintain the property.

5. Non-hierarchical structure and decision-making: Leadership roles naturally exist in cohousing communities; however, no one person (or persons) has authority over others.

6. No shared community economy: The community is not a source of income for its members.

Due to the negative connotations that intentional communities received during the 1960-70s, there are some members of cohousing communities who do not like to be defined as intentional communities. It is true that there are varying levels of intentionality in communities; however, cohousing communities are by definition classified as intentional communities. It may be helpful to acknowledge that Songaia emerged out of a more traditional form of intentional community, yet chose to build using the cohousing model and meet the criteria.

Finally, as you encounter these stories from my family-in-community, from friends and neighbors I love, I ask the reader to receive them with a spirit of openness. Respecting and accepting people as they are, that's the gift of community.

Fred Lanphear
September 2010

Songaia Through the Seasons

This is a quick view into what it's like to live a kid's life in Songaia.
Each season is unique in its own way to our community.

Spring!

I joyfully run outside. It's warm enough to play outside a lot now!
I am quickly soaked by the early morning dew. I hear infant birds
calling for food, and think of baby animals in their burrows. The
flowers are opening their petals. A cloud darkens the sky, and soon
misty rain is falling down, watering flowers and the beds of soon-
to-be planted gardens. The Songaians are eager to plant the gardens
before the upcoming Earth Day festival. I hear the humming of lawn
mowers in the distance, as people desperately try to battle the weeds
before long days begin. A "V" of geese passes over the cloudy sky,
honking noisily, heading for home. Sunshine signals summer is near.

Summertime!

The scent of the fresh cut lawn and watermelons wafts deliciously
over the community. I run laughing across the field, tall grass whipping
my legs and scratching me. Heat wafts over me, but I am cooled down
immediately by the water fight that I join. After that, we head over to
the common house where people like to hang out, where the smell of
hot dogs, watermelon, and Popits® flows through the air. After I have
my fill of watermelon, I head over to the forest and participate in some
of the dry leaf fights, with kids screaming and yelling, throwing leaves
at each other. I am happy, because there is no school, which means I
can go to dinner at the common house every night! I get thirsty, so I
go and have some lemonade, along with another slice of watermelon.
As soon as I near the tables, the smells of the grill wash over me. A
plane buzzes softly overhead. I run back, filling up my water gun. A
dragonfly darts overhead, as an air conditioner starts whirring softly.
As I run, I hear Tom yelling "AMELIA!", attempting to call his
daughter home. As I suck blueberries, munch on raspberries, I hear
the crickets chirp. As a leaf falls off a tree, I realize it will soon be fall.

Fall!

The kids reluctantly shuffle toward their first day of school. As the rain starts pouring from the sky, I think about fresh apples, and the bears starting hibernation. The colorful leaves highlight everywhere they touch, and crackle under my feet. After school, I stomp through the tall grass, enjoying myself until dinner. After dinner, we prepare pumpkins for Halloween and set up decorations! I eagerly ask my parents if I can go candy shopping. They say yes, and off we go. I shiver in the cold air, reflecting that winter is almost upon us.

Winter!

Snow falls softly, muffling most noise. The bare trees stand skeletal against the white, some with bird feeders hanging from them, but not very many birds eat from them. A few frozen streams leave baleful outlines in the snow. The sound of screaming from sledding and snowball fights slices through the icy air. One sled goes careening toward a snow fort; then, in a spray of snow, screams of Aaaahhhhh! And mittens, they collide. A kid flies through the air, with a bewildered expression on his face, which quickly turns to one of horror as he looks below him and lands in a pile of icy snowballs. I quickly hurry inside for some hot chocolate, because one of my gloves just froze!

My community, Songaia, undergoes many changes through every season. It's a nice place to live through the entire year.

—Lucas Kershner

CHAPTER TWO

Journey of Self-Development

The dream of Songaia Cohousing Community emerged in the early 1990s out of an existing intentional community when cohousing was just taking root in the U.S. The community, called the Residential Learning Center (RLC), was in transition and the cohousing model offered an exciting concept for creating a meaningful neighborhood. Over the next ten years the community evolved through the process of organizing, planning, designing and ultimately building their community structure and facilities.

Stages of Community Formation

Residential Learning Center

The RLC was the program center of the Institute of Cultural Affairs (ICA), focused on holistic education and rites of passage for youth. The ICA is a not-for-profit organization that began as a program division of the Ecumenical Institute in the 1970s. The ICA's primary objective is to promote positive change in communities, organizations and the lives of individuals by helping people find their own solutions to problems and the means to implement those solutions.

Initially the RLC consisted of two to three staff families that lived communally with 9 to 11 youths, between the ages of 12 and 14. The youth program center was originally located in

Chicago and moved to Seattle in 1986, so that it could be more focused on care for the earth. The land was purchased in the fall of 1986 and was rezoned to permit the property to be used as a group home. The youth and staff moved in during 1987. The youths participated in local schools and were involved in after-school activities at the RLC, such as gardening, meal preparation, theater productions, celebrations, etc. In their 9th grade year, they went overseas to participate in ICA projects where they experienced another culture and were initiated into global citizenship. The youth program was discontinued in 1990 due to financial constraints. The two staff families remaining, Stan and Carol Crow, and Fred and Nancy Lanphear and son Bob, 28, began the process of re-visioning the future.

The title of the first five acres (called the North Five) was in the name of two of the original staff families, the Crows and Coffmans. The Coffmans left in 1989. The second five acres (called the South Five), that was included as an option to purchase on the first five acres, was purchased by the ICA in 1989. The staff families that remained on the property and others who moved into the community were covering the mortgages of both properties. This contributed to increasing the property equity that would eventually be used in obtaining bank financing for the construction loan. Each property had dwellings, and the one on the North Five was built out to house up to 12 youths, so it had many bedrooms. Individuals and families interested in living cooperatively were recruited to become members of the intentional community. As folks joined, they could decide to be part of the visioning process as well as be immersed in the economic and social life of the community.

How Songaia Got Its Name

The time was late winter or early spring in 1991 and the place was the Residential Learning Center (RLC) in Bothell, Washington. Three youths were a part of the RLC at that time, and that evening they had joined the adults living here for the express purpose of creating a new name for this beautiful 11 acres in Canyon Park. The RLC was coming to a close and the new vision was to create a cohousing community.

We gathered in the living room, youths on their bellies on the floor, and we agreed we would not leave until the job was accomplished. We first talked about what characteristics or images we wanted represented in the name. Music, sun, Earth were a few that emerged. Some combinations were in Spanish, as in Casa something. After an hour or so of thinking and stating many possibilities without success, in frustration we went to the kitchen where ice cream sundaes were served to crystallize the spirits.

Clearly, people continued thinking while they ate and upon our return to the living room, we resumed. Soon Bob Lanphear, on staff with the RLC, in a hesitant voice and obviously grasping for the right combination began… "How about Song… song…gaia…SONGAIA! We each said it a few times, looked at each other and said, "That's IT!"

Within 20 minutes, everyone returned to their rooms, pleased as punch and firm in the realization that Songaia, which can be interpreted as "Song of the Living Earth," was who we were and how we wanted to be known down through the years. Our community had once again pooled its wisdom and created a symbolic name for a new entity coming into being.

—Carol Crow

During this early transitional stage there were between 15 to 25 individuals living on the property at any one time, proportionately dividing mortgage costs, maintenance and living expenses, based on space utilized and number of individuals in the family. Some families had children, so we were multi-generational from the beginning. A few of the early members were interested in becoming members of the cohousing community and some were not. All were interested in and committed to living cooperatively.

We shared a common kitchen and ate all of our evening meals together, taking turns preparing the meal and cleaning up. Breakfast and lunch were prepared individually or by families from the same kitchen. There was a common pantry. We each had our private rooms but shared bathrooms, living room and other common spaces. Because of the intensity of our living arrangements it was essential that we meet regularly to organize the practices of cooperative living and work out our issues. The schedule that worked for us in this stage of our community living was to hold two house meetings and one sharing circle per month. Although many of these individuals did not become part of the cohousing community, they each contributed to the unfolding dream in various unique and significant ways.

Pre-cohousing Community Forms

The first new family to eventually become members of the current cohousing community, Craig Ragland, Karly Lubach and their 9-year old son, Zeph, moved onto the property in the fall of 1992. Tom Barr and Michelle Grandy, who are currently cohousing members, began meeting with us as early as 1993 and continued through the extended self-development process, but did not move onto the property until after the new units were built. There were others who joined earlier but did not continue through the total process. Another current member family, Chuck and Marilyn Hanna-Myrick, moved onto the property in 1996. There were four others who moved onto the property with the intent of being members, but opted to leave before construction.

The dynamics of having a portion of the forming community living on the property during the development stages were both positive and negative. On the positive side, it symbolized a sense of seriousness and permanence, particularly as one of the families sold their home before moving in. It also contributed to the experience of living in community as a preview and anticipation of what was to come. A negative value may have been that the urgency of completion may not have been as great for those living on the land. There also may have been a perception of an inside and outside group, although this never was articulated as a serious issue.

Pre-move-in Songaia Cohousing Community

The forming community went through many comings and goings that will be described later in this chapter. As we approached the final stages of completing our financing prior to construction, we had 10 member families. The final three families joined us during construction.

During the six month construction period we existed as a scattered community. During this period all of the families living on the property moved into some form of temporary dwellings for varying periods of time. Most of these families rented apartments. Nancy and I stayed on the property during construction for all but one month. We worked closely with the project manager in handling property questions and were ready to protect existing trees from being damaged or destroyed. We eventually had to move when all utilities were shut off.

During the construction period we met monthly at a nearby church, where we had potluck dinners followed by a meeting. We worked hard at creating some semblance of being a community during this phase. At our last meeting in the church before we moved in, we simulated being a community by celebrating trick or treat at Halloween by stationing families alternately at two doors, and the kids would go back and forth to play trick or treat with each family as they took their turn answering the door.

Chronology of Development

In the Spring of 1990, the residential staff of the ICA envisioned the transformation of their mission to encompass the following four arenas:

1. Research and development of new patterns appropriate to a biocentric, eco-spiritual community, including cohousing as a primary strategy.
2. Intensification of a multi-generational, co-learning community of individuals and families participating in their own conscious evolution and related lifestyles.
3. Design and implementation of replicable rites of passage that signify transition of the life journey within a biocentric mythology.
4. Documentation and networking with other organizations concerned with education, the environment, multi-cultural understanding and human development.

Within this framework, the Songaia Cohousing Community was born. The first year was a time of research and formulation of strategies for the transition from an intentional, corporately owned community to equity-based housing using the cohousing concept.

Vision and Value Statement

The basic decision to form a multigenerational cohousing community evolved quickly and smoothly. The co-founding families had lived for many years in shared housing situations that could be described as intense and frequently less than desirable living conditions. When one of our members, who had recently been to a cohousing presentation, described this new type of intentional community, it was an "aha" moment for us. There was no question about whether it would be an adult community or multi-generational. Both of the initial families had been involved in child-centered educational programs and were committed to including children.

The values were generated over a number of sessions, mostly by folks living in the community at the time. Prior to these sessions, we participated in a common study of *The Dream of the Earth* by Thomas Berry. This book formed our thinking along with the values and principles we brought from our ICA and individual pasts. The brief version of our seven values is as follows:

1. We value living lightly on the land, considering how our decisions will affect the land and people in coming generations.
2. We value a rich spirit life in community, emerging from our total and varied life experiences.
3. We honor the individual, family and community, and seek ways to balance the needs of each.
4. We encourage life-long learning, acknowledging that each person, regardless of age, is a contributor and recipient of learning.
5. We respect and celebrate the variety of cultures and backgrounds our community encompasses.
6. We seek to share responsibility and contributions from all our members.
7. We value a sense of mission or service beyond our local community, connecting us to the larger community and the world.

Initial Planning, Organizational Framework and Timeline

We began actively promoting and recruiting members to our planning process at the Puget Sound Cohousing Fair in April 1991. In a one-year period we grew from a founding group of three families to nine families who were considered full partners in the Songaia development process. Full partnership in this early stage had a minimal financial commitment of $2,000, with an initial payment of $200 and the remaining due as needed. The time commitment was beginning to become substantial. We met twice a month for 3.5 to 4 hours each time. In addition, there were nine committees that met as needed to research and formulate models.

A timeline in 1992 projected completion in 1995. This was overly ambitious and, in retrospect, naïve without the assistance of professional developers to guide us. We were modeling ourselves in relation to Winslow Cohousing Community on Bainbridge Island and Puget Ridge Cohousing in West Seattle, both of which had professional developers as part of their membership. It took us twice as long as we had anticipated. The 10-year timeline described the chronology of primary activities, financing, use of consultants, major achievements and fluctuations in membership.

The extended timeline may have had some benefits, such as the increase in the equity of the property as the mortgage was gradually reduced from rental income, as well as the outright payment of the mortgage by a few members. Another benefit was the sense of achievement and of community that developed among those who remained on the journey until completion. A downside was the loss of members who lost patience with the slow progress of the process.

Development Process

The participative process was focused on four action arenas: 1) formation, 2) site development, 3) building development and 4) community patterns. As we did not have consultants to guide us in the early stages, we included common study as part of our meeting time. The two books we studied were: 1) *Cohousing: A Contemporary Approach to Housing Ourselves* by Kathryn Mc-Camant and Charles Durett and 2) *Pattern Language* by Christopher Alexander, et al. As we looked ahead, we projected four levels of development: 1) initial site design, 2) feasibility study/

common area site design, 3) pre-zoning permit application design, and 4) zoning compliance planning and pre-construction design modifications. Each of these had multiple steps to complete. A comprehensive model for the development process was in place. The four development arenas were sub-divided into major components under which action steps were listed.

Development Program

The 31-page Development Program document printed in the summer of 1994 was the coalescence of the hopes, dreams and visions of a group of about 15 persons over a three-year period. It represented a deep understanding of the land, ourselves as a community, and many resulting complex relationships to the site, housing and common facilities. It became our handbook as we continued to give form to our unfolding dream.

The Development Program consisted of the following components:

1. An overview of our community: its present and its future
2. Our ecological perspective
3. Relationship to the surrounding land and neighbors
4. Accessibility
5. Site Program
6. Housing Program
7. Common House Program
8. Affordability

The Community Development Program Document

The community development program document was my first task. In fact, the community bought me my first CAD program. And with that I could start developing the site plan, and they commissioned me to produce this document. This was probably two or three months of work, a lot of interviewing, a lot of research with the county and with looking at the codes as well as a number of introductory programming meetings where we'd try to figure out how many units, how large the units would be, the spirit of the units, the different types of general configurations, how many bedrooms, and otherwise the site limitations on the property and the number of units and all that. Septic versus sewer; well, there was no sewer at the time so we had to go septic, and what kind of limitations that imposed on us. And then a big portion of this was about our values, where to build on the land, where not to build on the land.

We went through a number of discernment exercises, where we walked the land. We looked at the land from the standpoint of views, view corridors, sacred spaces, private spaces, natural resources that we wanted to preserve, and then maybe open spaces or public spaces. And from just that early site surveying, we were able to map different zones based on those characteristics. That went some way towards informing a real early, primitive site plan as far as where we might build and where we were forbidden to build. That's shown in the Community Development Program document: view corridors, for example, where the gardens would go, where the children might like to play.

At the same time we were working on site planning, and ideas were emerging. We learned that we could only have 13 units. Where would the common house be located? The kind of formulaic site-planning strategy for co-housing out of Denmark is to organize the development around the street. So they had these linear axes with houses on both sides. And they put a couple of mini streets together, and where they come together forms a knuckle, and that's usually where the common house is located. Well, we had to forgo that model when we made the decision that the existing big house, a 5,000 square foot rambler, would become our common house. This was one of many decisions we had to make that challenged some of the design values we would strive for.

—Tom Barr

Conceptual Plans and Rezoning Application

The first conceptual plans were prepared in 1991 by Bob Lanphear, an architectural designer and an early member of the cohousing community. These plans projected triplexes, duplexes and stand-alone units as well as a common house all connected by foot paths and interspersed with landscaping.

A revised conceptual design was prepared by Bob in conjunction with Tom Barr, also an architectural designer who joined us in 1992. The revised design consisted of six duplexes, a single stand-alone unit, plus the common house, which was our understanding of the maximum we could locate on the land using a community-based septic system. The single unit was later folded into the south end of the common house as a way of reducing costs. The design was developed and included in our work on our Development Program described above. This provided us the plan that was used to apply for rezoning.

Go, with God Speed

We had a committee called the Shepprds. The "prd" was for Planned Residential Development so they called us the "Shepprds," or the PRDs for short. They commissioned me to head up the PRD effort at an annual meeting. I was to put a basic site plan together, work with a civil engineer, put the PRD package together and whisk it to Snohomish County, submit it and shepherd it on through. They fashioned some winged shoes I was to put on and gave me a staff that I would wave around and go quickly, with God speed.

Fred worked closely with me, and we did move quickly. I remember there was much ceremony and fanfare in my send-off, if you will, to head up this effort. Because getting the PRD involved getting the zoning changed and getting it changed to a planned residential community. That involved zoning changes, justifying the zoning changes, putting in for the PRD, justifying the PRD, and a hearing and en-

vironmental review. And we were determined not to have a negative impact on the environment.

—Tom Barr

Achieving approval from Snohomish County to build a planned residential development (PRD) on the land was perceived as the first major hurdle. The PRD would allow us to increase the number of homes we could place on the property as well as clustering them without subdividing the land into multiple lots. We made many trips to the Community Development and Planning office to see a variety of officials. Fortunately, we found a county staff member that had been to a presentation about cohousing who understood and was extremely supportive of the concept and of our proposal. We experienced her as an advisor as well as an advocate as she navigated us through the complexities of county regulations. What we didn't know as we went through all the requirements for submitting our rezone proposal was that the clock was running out on what we wanted to do. Three months after we submitted our application for rezone, the Growth Management Act (GMA) was approved. If we had waited three more months we would have had to meet very different requirements. We were "grandfathered in" under the zoning requirements that were in place before the GMA was approved.

The GMA designated our property to be in an urban growth area with high housing density requirements. We did not fully understand the implications of this new zoning act until the municipal sewer lines were installed and the developers began to purchase all the land they could. They then started building house after house on very small lots. Under this zoning act, we would have been required to have a much higher density than we did.

"How Do They Know?"

It was the big day of our land use hearing. About 15 of us went into the hearing room where the Hearing Examiner presided. He turned out to be extremely cordial and patient with us because this was very unorthodox for do-it-yourselfers to show up at a zoning hearing and propose what they wanted to do with their land. Usually there would be professional engineers and architects that were advocating on behalf of the client. But today it was just me, on the stand, decked out in suit and tie, speaking on behalf of Songaia.

I remember there was this one point at which there was a technical consideration about the growth management boundary and our project's relationship to it. The commissioner was not grilling me, but was asking me a technical question about whether I believed that our project fell under the category of some zoning principle and therefore should be permitted because of this or that and this exclusion and that exception. I didn't know what to tell him. I didn't know whether to tell him yes or no. I kind of glazed over and froze on the stand. I looked over at our group and saw some nodding "yes" and others mouthing the word "yes," and I'm thinking to myself "How do they know? I mean, if I don't know the answer to the question, how could they possibly know the answer to the question?" I had studied all this stuff.

"Well, it turns out, I learned afterwards, they had all been following the cues from our contact in the County Planning Office, who was also present. She knew the answer to the question, and was nodding "yes," but I couldn't see her because there was a building column between us. But since our group said "yes!" I said, "Yes! That's exactly what we mean!" And the rest of the hearing just kind of sailed right through, and the Hearing Examiner took our answer as our declaration of the legal framework under which we were making our claim to develop. But, I tell you, to this day I can't really fully explain the zoning framework under which we exist!

—Tom Barr

Recruiting, Attrition and Continued Recruitment

Recruiting folks to join in creating the Songaia dream was the first order of business. The founding members were very clear about the importance of engaging future members in the planning process from the outset. One of the initial strategies was to write and invite former ICA colleagues to join us, naively thinking they would be very receptive to the cohousing concept as a creative modification of their former mode of communal living. We did not get any positive responses and discovered later that most of our colleagues did not have intentional community in their future plans.

Fortunately, the cohousing concept had been introduced in the Puget Sound in the late '80s and had attracted a significant number of followers. We discovered very early that there were other groups in different stages of forming cohousing community. In fact, one of the first events for Songaia to go public was at a Puget Sound Cohousing Fair in the spring of 1991. This was a wonderful opportunity to share our vision and invite folks to visit and or join us. In this first year, our numbers increased from three families to seven families, although only two of the founding families remained to move into the finished community. The following year, five new families joined, while three dropped out. The remaining nine families were consistently involved for the next two to three years and were primarily responsible for the basic design of the houses and the layout of the community.

In 1994, a new member joined and one left, so that we were still at nine. In 1995 we had five new families join us and two leave, increasing our community to eleven. In 1996, a 12th family joined us, putting us near to being full. That was also the year that we got the first cost estimate from the contractor that came in so very high. It was a very discouraging time for us and contributed to six families leaving before the end of the year, cutting our membership in half. It was like starting all over again.

One family returned in early 1997, only to leave for the second time after another two years. Two more families joined in 1998, three more in 1999, and the final three during construction. During construction we had more wanting to join than we had spaces.

Recruitment, or marketing, took place in a variety of ways: through our website, at local cohousing fairs, in classified ads in the Puget Sound Consumers Cooperative monthly newsletter, articles in various media, and probably most effectively by word of mouth and personal connections. Our recruiting efforts intensified as we got into the last three to four years, particularly after we lost half our members in 1996.

Creative Financing

Soft development costs were very modest in the first three years and were funded by small loans from some of the early members of the forming team. They were called loans because they earned 9% annual interest. These funds covered the initial feasibility study and legal fees for incorporating as the Songaia Cooperative.

Once we were incorporated in 1994, we were in a position to purchase the South Five from the ICA. The property was appraised and we purchased it at market value. A down payment of $15K was required. At the same time, the ICA family whose names were on the title for the North Five requested that their names be removed so they would be free of any encumbrances that would prevent them from purchasing a home in their new location. This provided the opportunity of re-financing the North Five and adding the other co-founding family to the title. This provided the project with $53,000 that was made available for covering the South Five down payment and for additional soft development costs which were soon to intensify.

It should be noted that the only increase in the original cost of the land that was passed on as a cost to cohousing members was the annual 9% interest earned by the original cofounding family on the original down payment they had made on the property. In 1997, it became necessary to pay off the mortgage so we could turn over 10 feet of frontage road at our entry road to the county. To accomplish this, two additional families that were now living on the property along with the cofounding families contributed $253,000 to finalize the purchase. The four families now owned the property as tenants-in-common, adding two families to the previous tenants-in-common ownership arrangement.

Hiring a development consultant and an architect in 1996 required additional funds. It was at this stage in our development that we decided to raise the amount of advances per member to $6,000 and then $7,000. The agreement was that this would be reimbursed if the member decided to leave, but only if there was a new member to purchase their shares, and this would only happen after all the units had been pre-sold. This protected our funds from being unexpectedly depleted. Some of the new members did not have sufficient liquid assets to make the required advances. One of the families with additional liquid assets arranged to provide personal loans to them at 7% interest.

In 1998 it was necessary to request an additional $6,000 per member to cover our increasing development costs and again in 1999 to cover attorney costs to re-incorporate us as a condominium association. It was recommended that we structure ourselves legally as a condominium association because as a cooperative we would have to pay a higher interest on our construction loan and would be required to have pre-sold all of the units. We knew this might happen when we initially chose to be a cooperative, so the decision to change legal forms did not come as a shock.

It was becoming clear by 1996 that our financial feasibility was shaky. The county requirements for managing storm water runoff, roads and parking, and the cost of building our community-based septic system was excessively elevating our infrastructure costs, which could only be allocated across the maximum number of 13 units the county would allow us to build. The primary strategies for addressing the issue of financial viability were: 1) increasing the equity that could be put into the project, 2) reducing the costs that would be covered in the construction loan, and 3) obtaining a construction bid that allowed us to keep our costs under the appraised value of the project.

A major factor contributing to feasibility was the $635,000 in equity we accumulated going into the project. Most of this was from the value of the North Five property that had been acquired in 1986 and paid for by renters over a 10-year period, with the final payment in 1997 by outright purchase by four member families—the Crows, Lanphears, Ragland-Lubach, and Hanna-Myricks—and then transferred to the new community at cost. The appraised equity value was significantly higher because the appraised value of the property had significantly increased. Renovating the existing residential unit on the South Five using personal labor also increased its equity value, incurring only material costs.

Cost reduction strategies were used whenever possible. One of these strategies was what we called "off-mortgage projects," most of which were modifications to the Common House to be in compliance with the commercial building codes. We made these changes ourselves rather than including it as part of the construction contract. This included elevating the floor in the dining room, rebuilding a deck railing, and re-hanging exterior doors so they opened outwards.

What To Do with the Barn?

Early in our development, we had a University of Washington architectural class spend a whole semester studying our project as a case study. One team looked into the feasibility of the barn becoming a

Common House. They found that the inherent structure and the nature of the barn were not suited to be weatherized as an occupied structure. So we abandoned the idea. Actually the barn would've been too big of a Common House for just 13 units. At that point we came up with the divided Common House concept: those activities that are all-weather, sloppy or dusty, could be done in the barn, but the activities that require warmth, intimacy, containment and stability could be done in a portion of the 5000-square-foot house that was to become our Common House.

Nobody wanted to tear the barn down, even though we tossed the idea around. Once we made the decision that we were going to keep the barn, we knew it had one Achilles' heel, and that was the roof. It was rusty, but it was just surface rust. We actually rented a sandblasting machine, donned the sandblasting outfits, and totally sandblasted the surface of the barn's roof. Roger, one of our early members, a professional painter, came in with his paint-spraying outfit and sprayed the roof.

Fred came up with the idea of scaling the barn down by enclosing the open front with lattice to create a bicycle storage area and passageway. The other ugly feature of the barn was the old fiberglass attached greenhouse. Perhaps fortuitously, a big storm came and collapsed the roof on it. We had to rebuild practically the entire greenhouse, and it was at that point that we located recycled, double-paned windows that were used to rebuild the greenhouse. We then extended the greenhouse into a lattice-enclosed toy storage area. These modifications served to scale the barn down so that it isn't so severe.

The barn kind of defined us early on: because it was this kind of utilitarian metal building and we decided to keep it, there would be this kind of rag-tag, scruffy side to us that was a pragmatic, do-it-yourself style. The barn helped to steer us away from the totally sanitized view of a new cohousing community. We were more rough and ready and willing to make compromises in order to live out our basic values, that was connection to the Earth, and to some extent frugality.

—Tom Barr

Legal Configurations

From the beginning, the decision about legal form was not made easily. As we considered the alternatives, starting in 1993, we found ourselves torn between going with a condominium association, a form that was well-recognized by banks, and a cooperative, a form that had limited recognition by banks, but was more closely aligned with our values and practices. We spent considerable time and energy to compare and ultimately decide our legal form.

To Be or Not To Be

Soon after we got involved, in 1992, I either got recruited or volunteered to be on the legal committee where we had to start taking the first steps towards concretization. I remember that the earliest organizational notion was that we'd be a cooperative. I think we even incorporated as a cooperative. But I think even before that, there was debate about should we be a cooperative or a condo. So I remember going to Seattle Public Library and getting a whole bunch of books on cooperative structure. I brought all these books home, and I said "Well, we have got to read these books." And nobody really wanted to read the books. But I read the books, and it seemed like a cooperative held our values most precisely as far as being able to choose membership.

—Tom Barr

A major difference between the two legal forms was that as a cooperative we would have some decision power regarding membership, whereas a condominium did not. Our concern was attracting members that were aligned to our values and community living principles and practices. Another difference that attracted us to a cooperative was the option of interchanging portions or whole units among members without going through a real estate transaction using the mechanism of adjustment of shares. The primary downside of cooperatives was they did not have the credibility in the marketplace that condominium associations had.

We solicited opinions from existing cohousing communities based on their experience and at one point convened a panel discussion on choosing the most appropriate legal form. This brought together representatives from other forming communities to interact with a representative from a bank, an association that supports cooperatives, and from an association of intentional communities. The pros and cons were discussed and we were left to decide for ourselves which option would best meet our needs. Of the many comments that were made, one that seemed poignant was, "You will be making many compromises as you go through this process, do not compromise until it is essential." After considerably more research we decided to incorporate as a cooperative.

We hired the one attorney in Seattle who was experienced and most qualified to guide us in the process of incorporating as a cooperative. We were given instructions on how to create our Articles of Incorporation and Bylaws. This took months of dialogue interspersed with meetings with our attorney. Finally, in early 1994, we completed and submitted our application for incorporation. We received our incorporation papers and held a grand signing celebration with a notary public that we coaxed to be present so we could do this officially as a group.

The Biggest Controversy

The biggest controversy of all during our development process centered on the concept of limited equity. This was a tough one. Many of us held the value that housing should not be a commodity that appreciates speculatively. We wanted housing at Songaia to be decoupled from the speculative housing market in some way. So the idea of limited equity emerged: When you buy your house, you pay a certain original price, but thereafter, instead of the market determining the selling price, an agreed-upon formula would govern. Early drafts of the limited equity policy used the Consumer Price Index as the escalating factor. So, if you wanted to sell your house, you'd look back at what you paid for it, how many years you held it, and from that derive the appreciation you are allowed.

Fred was very much the advocate of a restrictive appreciating factor. Other members, however, were asking, "What if I buy my house here at Songaia, then find that the community is not for me, and I really need to move out? I want to be able to take my equity in Songaia and move to an equivalent house somewhere else without penalty. And, I don't want Songaia limiting how much I can get for my house, causing me to suffer a loss." Still other members didn't care much at all. They just wanted to live in community. The resulting discussions about limited equity got very heated. We were stuck.

I found myself in this intermediary position. I was sympathetic to the limited equity concept, but I thought Fred's factor was a little too restrictive. So the Navigators, the community steering committee, told Fred and me that if we wanted limited equity, we'd have to work it out and come up with a clear, agreeable formula. At the time, there was a fellow in the group, Steve Leopold, whose forte was business and finance and he really understood these concepts. He thought the CPI was not appropriate for limiting home equity because it included the costs of all commodities, not just housing. He found a housing-specific index: Net Effective Rent. This is a government index published for major U.S. cities. The government and real estate businesses use it to predict the escalation of rents. So, Fred and I, after much hand-wringing deliberation, settled on this approach, took it to the community, and said, "This is what we think it needs to be." The community accepted this formula, but probably mostly out of exhaustion. It turned out that we eventually lost a couple of members—partly, I believe, as a result of this decision.

The ironic twist came a few months later. Deborah Gooden, our development consultant, came to us and said, "You know the limited equity provisions that you wrote into your documents? Well, the Coop Bank has changed its policy and is not buying it. You have to get rid of it." Now, having become much more pragmatic, we took it back to the group and it didn't take us more than 10 minutes to kiss limited equity goodbye. Above all else, we had to keep the project moving.

—Tom Barr

We did business as a cooperative until 1999, when our development consultant encouraged us to shift to a condominium association in order to have greater financial flexibility. We were very concerned about whether we were financially viable at this stage of our journey and quickly made the decision to shift, even though it would cost another $10,000 in legal fees. The attorney was sensitive to our values and helped us prepare our bylaws in a way that was in line with our values. For example, every member in the association is on the board of directors so that all of the decisions belong to all of us.

Just prior to becoming a homeowners condominium the attorney had us incorporate as an LLC. This allowed us to function as a group until all the units were purchased and we became a homeowners association. As long as we were an LLC we also had the power to choose who became members. The actual time frame of the LLC was months and not years.

The condominium association legal form has worked well for us. Our earlier concern about members joining us that were not suited to community living has not been an issue that would have been addressed by being a cooperative. We have only had two units that have been sold, and in both cases the new members were actively seeking to be in community. The process of self-selection seems to work.

Professional Assistance

As a self-developed cohousing community, we only accessed professional help as it was needed. We did not have professionals guiding us from the beginning to the end and none of the professionals we hired had experience working with cohousing communities. One could reasonably argue that the timeline for the development process would have been greatly shortened if we had worked with cohousing professionals.

Other than a brief consultation with an attorney about legal forms, the first intensive use of professionals was contracting a feasibility study. This was accomplished in 1992 by a real estate developer and a planning consultant who worked together to investigate the county requirements and projected costs to ascertain if our proposed project was actually feasible. They found that the project was feasible, assuming the existing residences would be sold to members. A second feasibility study was done again in 1994 by a developer who was involved with cohousing. It confirmed the earlier study that the project was feasible.

The next intensive use of a professional was the hiring of Jan Bianchi, an attorney who guided us in incorporating as a housing cooperative. This took considerable time, as we took on the task of writing the articles and bylaws ourselves. The attorney reviewed and corrected these as an ongoing process. Her processing time was as slow as ours so the end product was a long time in coming.

The professional assistance that was most critical came from our financial development consultant, Deborah Gooden, who was recommended to us by the National Cooperative Bank (NCB). Since we were incorporated as a housing cooperative, we intended NCB to finance our project. She had worked for the NCB and was one of the few consultants available with that background. We hired her in 1996 and our planning process immediately accelerated. She connected us with a registered architect, Rick Brown, who we needed in order for banks to look at our project drawings. She also introduced us and encouraged us to utilize a design-build approach to planning. Under this model the architect and the contractor collaborate to ensure that the final design is doable within an affordable price range. We approved both the architect and contractor she recommended.

It Was Great To Be Just One of the Community

True to our spirit, we did everything ourselves except what we really had to farm out. That was our development plan. We didn't do the traffic study, nor did we do the septic design. But I was an intern architect and a part of me really wanted to run with this exciting project. In the end, I decided against it. And that was actually a very good decision because there's no way I could make the separation between the role of the client and that of the architect.

As a member of a forming community, you bring hopes, dreams, aspirations and specific goals and needs to the group. And in my case, I brought them passionately, like "I think we ought to do this!" But the architect's role is to listen to all this passion and then say, "Well, you know, I hear everything you're saying, but based on your budget, the site, and the time-line, you can afford this and this, but you can't afford this and this over here."

It was really difficult for me to bring objectivity to it all. I was thinking of taking the job to the firm that I was working for. I talked it over with my boss, and he warned me against it. And the community talked a lot about it. I was relieved when we finally made the decision to hire an independent architect. It was a great decision—to hire it out—because designing a community, "hands-on" as we did, is such an intense experience. Relieved of the architectural role, I could just be one of the community.

—Tom Barr

We soon discovered that the design-build concept did not work for us. The architect and contractor either did not meet with each other as was intended, or one or the other was not working within our financial restrictions. The first estimate from the contractor was unbelievably high and the second estimate, after major changes in the design were made to bring the project where it could be financed, was still $600,000 over budget. We realized that contractors had more work than they could handle, so it was not surprising that the estimates were high. We decided to look for another contractor.

It was at this point that our development consultant suggested we ask contractors to look at our architectural plans and tell us if they thought they could provide us a bid that would be within our budgeted amount set by the bank appraisal on our project. Three construction companies said they could, so we interviewed all three and narrowed the companies to two. They were given a timeframe in which to complete the bid. One company came in $300,000 over budget with provisions for lowering the cost with changes we would have to make. The other company, Gemkow Construction, came within budget and we decided to go with them. Not only were they within budget, they said they could complete construction in six months. This was crucial because it would reduce the amount of daily interest we would be paying on our construction loan.

Other professionals that were brought into the planning and development process included the attorney, Joe McCarthy, who helped us re-incorporate as a condominium association; David Dougherty, a civil engineer who designed our storm water drainage system to meet county requirements; and a septic system engineer, Craig Schuck, who not only designed our community septic system but periodically checks the system to make sure it is working properly.

Professionals were a critical part of our development team. Selecting ones who could align themselves with our community's values and intent was essential. Each carry their own biases, so it was important to find those who could flex to meet our particular want and needs. The selection process for each of the professionals was one of the unglamorous, but critical tasks, in the overall process. In certain instances, it was not the primary professional we hired, but one of their subordinates that played a key role, as was the case with the construction company we hired. The on-site project manager, Jeff Doran, became a working partner during the construction phase, helping us to preserve trees, assuring construction quality and being flexible when needed. As a community, we are very conscious and grateful of the role they performed in partnership with us.

Pre-construction Projects

One advantage of the protracted self-development journey was the time it provided us to make permanent improvements on the property. Many of these were critical to our ability to function as a community, and others added to the value and aesthetics of the community. These included building the dining/meeting room in the common house, renovation of Unit 1, renovation of the propagation house, the barn makeover, and construction of an external stairway in the Common House.

Common House Renovations

It is not surprising that our first major project was to convert the carport of the future Common House into our dining/meeting room. As our numbers grew it became critical that we have adequate space for our meetings. The carport was the logical space, as it was large enough for the entire community to gather for meals and it was adjacent to the kitchen. Renovation included framing in the north and east walls, installing windows and exterior entry doors, lowering the open trusses to a regular ceiling with a vaulted ceiling in the center, and building a platform floor over the concrete floor. This took the combined efforts of resident and non-resident partners months to renovate. As we used this space for a few years before construction we became aware of a common problem in Common House dining rooms: noise. So, before we built we took on the project of adding acoustical tiles to the ceiling.

As we approached construction, we realized that we could reduce our cost by doing most of the common house renovation ourselves. One of the projects was building a new stairway in the back, connecting the kitchen to the laundry and guest rooms two stories below. Another was modifiying the deck railing to meet code requirements. Another was laying a new floor in the dinning room. This latter project was to meet code as well as refurbishing the disfigured flooring. A final project was refurbishing the kitchen cabinets.

Raising the Roof

When we decided to privatize the south end of the Common House, we lost the stairs between the main floor and the basement. Putting new stairs someplace else within the common house would take up too much space, so we decided to build some stairs on the outside of the common house. Tom, our resident architect, designed the open stairs, complete with a roof to protect us from the rain. It connected the narrow deck on the west that was accessible from the kitchen and living room to the basement door leading to the bathroom, guest rooms and laundry.

We worked together on workdays to build the roof and stairs. The roof required the erection of support columns and roof support joist. We built this assembly on the ground, and with the help of many hands, reminiscent of a barn-raising, we erected the assembly. Once up, it was a matter of extending the roof rafters out over the new support assembly.

The deck had to be shortened slightly to make room for the stairs, and then particular care was taken to keep the stairs evenly spaced when they were built.

—Chuck Hanna-Myrick

Renovation of Unit 1

The renovation of Unit 1 started in 1992 with reconstructing and shingling the roof. This structure was the original homestead, built piece-meal over many years starting in 1918. When the Lanphears chose this unit in 1992, it became essential to take immediate action on the roof. In 1994, work began on putting in a foundation and rebuilding the west and south walls. The renovation work continued over the next few years, including removing a fireplace and chimney and rebuilding the west wall when construction began. Most of the renovation work of Unit 1 was done by Fred and Nancy, with the help of Fred's brother, Perry, a contractor from the East Coast, and other community members.

Salvaging the Cottage

The oldest structure on the land was a single-story stucco dwelling that we called the "cottage." It was the original homestead on the property, with parts of it having been built around 1918. It had a massive stone fireplace out front and around back there was a little attached shed-roofed bathroom that was added on sometime long ago. The cottage was a total hodgepodge of construction. It was built out of gnarly studs with nothing plumb or level. Its few windows were severely weathered. The roof leaked, and the floor sagged. But Fred and Nancy couldn't bring themselves to demolish the house, you know, break it down, shovel it into a construction dumpster, send it to a landfill and start new. They insisted upon renovating it.

Well, Fred went into that house, and he damn near rebuilt the whole thing. He added a new roof structure, built a new bathroom, took off the stucco, installed new siding, and refinished the inside. I helped him a fair amount, and so did his brother, Perry, a contractor from RI who came out twice, spending a few weeks each time.

But the story I remember vividly is Fred taking the chimney down because it just didn't contribute anything anymore to the house. They would not need it for heating, as they were planning on a gas-stove unit. And, it took up the majority of the exterior wall of the living room, making it dark inside. Well, Fred started out—first he got a sledgehammer, and he tried to knock the rocks off and break the chimney up. But this chimney was like 8 feet wide and 20 feet high and the mortar was still really tough. He couldn't cut it with a sledgehammer. Then he went out, and he rented an electric jackhammer. And he pecked away at it for a couple of days, and he got frustrated. So then he went out, and he rented a full-blown, trailer-pulled, pneumatic jackhammer. And he made good progress with that. Finally, he eroded out the base of the chimney with that pneumatic jackhammer—enough that he then threw a rope around the top, hitched it to Doug's truck, and literally pulled the chimney over—a seismic event heard and felt by many.

—Tom Barr

Renovation of the Propagation House

One of the existing structures remaining from the time the property was a plant nursery was a corrugated fiberglass propagation house. It was attached to the barn on the west side and was not pleasing to look at. We decided to renovate it to make it more appropriate for a residential setting. We purchased large bay window units from a second-hand outlet and rebuilt the side-wall, installing the window units to maintain the greenhouse function. The roof was recovered with new corrugated fiberglass. This became necessary after a heavy snowstorm collapsed a portion of the roof. Benches were rearranged, a potting bench was built, and crushed rock was used to create a well-drained walking surface. When painted, it became a rather attractive building.

Barn Makeover

Unfortunately, the barn is the most imposing structure in the community. It serves us well or else it would have been removed long ago. In addition to its imposing size, the front of the barn was wide open so that everything was on display. It was an ugly sight. To reduce this negative visual impact we enclosed the front of the barn with solid panel wainscoting on the lower section and lattice on the upper section. It looks like an enclosed porch and greatly improves the appearance of the barn.

An interior modification of the barn was the addition of storage lofts. This required building an upper floor on the west wall of the barn 8' wide by 60' long. Three 20' storage areas were constructed by erecting 8' wire-mesh walls with a doorway opening in each. Each of these areas provided storage space for four units. The storage lofts were accessible by moving a mobile stairway into place.

Another interior modification was to create the food pantry for storing bulk food and food that needs to be refrigerated or frozen. This consisted of a room for freezers and refrigerators and a room to store dry and canned goods. The latter required extensive shelving and bin storage. The benefit of locating the bulk forage in the barn was twofold: reduced space demand on the Common House and more favorable ambient temperatures for food storage. These rooms were located under the storage lofts.

External Stairs on the Common House

The decision to privatize the south end of the Common House required that an additional stairway be constructed to provide access between floors on the north end. The most expedient and least invasive to existing space was to construct an external covered stairway. The stairway was attached to a back deck that was accessible from both the living room and the kitchen. We worked together to build the roof and stairs. The roof required the erection of support columns and roof support joist. We built this assembly on the ground, and with the help of many hands, reminiscent of a barn raising, we erected the assembly. Once up, it was a matter of extending the roof rafters out over the new support assembly.

The pre-construction projects contributed significantly to the appearance and marketability of the community while enhancing our sense of pride. The accomplishment of the pre-construction projects was a stepping stone towards achieving our ultimate goal and gave us encouragement in the extended process of development. They also helped us experience the power of our collected efforts and helped shape our community culture.

Building Community Culture During Development

Many of our current community patterns were established during the development stage. Singing, rituals and organizational structures, such as Navigators (our steering committee), were used during this period. Initially, the songs and rituals were a carryover from the ICA culture, but others were added as the partners grew beyond the founding family's influence. Consistency and discipline were foundational values and practices.

Some of our community's traditions were put in place during development, including observance of Solstice, Festival of the Earth, Thanksgiving, a weekend summer retreat, and our New Year's Eve celebration. Some of these events, such as the Festival of the Earth, served as a recruitment function. Others were designed as nurturing and sustaining events for "the long march."

The intensity and "staying power" in the extended duration of this stage of our life together was instrumental in building solidarity among the early members. We experienced many challenges, accomplishments and setbacks. We were continually reflecting on the spirit life of the community, particularly as partners left and new folks joined us.

We worked hard at creating a sense of identity and a sense of place. Our identity was enhanced by the choice of our name as we went through the transition from being the Residential Learning Center to becoming Songaia. The first logo we used was Songaia Cooperative but later printings were just Songaia. One of our members wrote new words to a song called "We Love the Mountains," changing it to "We love Songaia." Our sense of place was enhanced by work in the gardens and landscape as well as our continued use of the land for celebrations.

Final Financing, Construction and Move-in

Once we obtained an estimate that came in on budget, the final financing and construction phase went relatively quickly. We got approval from the bank for our $1.6 million construction loan in December 1999, started construction in April 2000, and moved in during October and November 2000. The community had been preparing itself for this final process for over nine years.

Marilyn was chosen as the "Owners Rep" to be the liaison with the contractor. She, along with Tom, Barb and Fred, worked as a team to make decisions on behalf of the community during the construction process. Decisions were made very quickly, as it was costing us hundreds of dollars a day in interest that would ultimately be factored into the total cost of the project. Each member of the team was overseeing different aspects of the process, including monitoring the finances, quality of construction, landscape management and the overall implementation process. Most decisions were made by the team without requiring consent from the total membership; some were made by the owners rep. In comparison to other stages in the development process, this was probably the smoothest and most efficient. There were no cost overruns and we stayed within budget and general time allowance. In fact there was a small surplus!

Fulfilling a Management Dream

As Songaia got ready to start construction, it became clear that we needed one person to speak for the group in dealing with the many professionals and handling questions, concerns, changes and the decision making that happens every day on a construction site. Waiting for 13 different unit owners to come up with answers would have created an impossible situation. When the backhoe operator has just severed the main line from the well to the irrigation system and water is squirting out, the consensus decision-making process is not the best way to determine whether to simply cap the leak or replace the pipe.

It turns out there was a term for the job of representing the owners and handling the communication with the architect, structural engineer, civil engineer, septic designer, hazmat coordinator, general contractor, lender, project coordinator and utility companies. The position is called the owners' representative or owners' rep for short. Songaia was ready to have one of those.

I agreed to take the job. I had joined Songaia in 1996. In 1997 I retired from my paid work as a librarian with the local county library system. My library gave me a party and a grand send off, but I left frustrated that I had not accomplished my professional goal of moving into management. I had plenty of free time and how hard could it be? I was about to find out.

We began construction in the spring of 2000. Present at the preconstruction meeting, April 17, 2000 were our architect, Rick Brown, our banker, Darel Grothaus, Mr. Grothaus's assistant, the general contractor's on-site manager, Jeff Doran and me. Our general contractor, Ed

Gemkow, was not present. Our various roles were established, the lines of communication drawn, and the place we planned to call home was basically off limits to most of us for the duration of the construction project.

And so we began. Every Monday there were site meetings when Rick Brown, Jeff Doran and I got together, walked the site and went over questions, change orders and problems. I also met weekly with a Songaia team consisting of Barb Bansensauer, Tom Barr, and Fred Lanphear, to go over what was happening on the owners' side on things. Barb handled all of the dealings with the lender and Tom provided his architectural expertise and detailed observation talents. He helped me to sound like I knew what I was talking about when I met with the professionals. I presented updates at our regular association meetings each month and worked with each of the unit owners in working on details specific to their unit. Periodically groups of us met with our development consultant, Deborah Gooden, to discuss obtaining our construction and mortgage loans, solve problems around interacting with various county department, and generally get pumped up to keep going.

Rick and I emailed, faxed and phoned each other constantly, often exchanging up to 20 messages each day. Questions about septic revisions, pathway lighting, the fire hydrant, bathroom fans, unit upgrades, heating in Common House dining room, the detention pond, pocket doors, hydroseeding, water meters and change orders flew back and forth. I had no idea that there were so many details to track in a project like ours. I got up early, stayed up late, woke up in the middle of the night worrying about what I might have forgotten, carried a cell phone constantly for the first time in my life and felt useful.

In November 2000 we got occupancy approval of all the units except for the combined common house and Unit 12. We celebrated Thanksgiving and moved in. My work as owners' rep continued in the early part of 2001, but with the completion of the common house and unit 12, I retired a second time from my volunteer owners' rep position.

Being the owners' rep was an incredible learning and growing experience for me. In preparation for writing this, I went to the Songaia archives and looked through the three file boxes of notes, sketches, site meeting minutes, bank draws, change orders, unit upgrades and other documents from the construction period of the Songaia history. Today, eight years later, I find it hard to believe all that I actually did. I learned so much about what goes into a construction project, what works and what can get messed up. I know details about what is under the ground on our property, in the walls of our houses, and on file with the county that few other people know. Whenever we cook a meal in our common kitchen, turn on a light in our houses, walk along our pathways or feel the warmth of our furnaces, I have the satisfaction of knowing that I contributed to making our physical existence on this land at this time possible. It was hard work, I stressed out a lot and I made many mistakes. I had my opportunity to manage, I appreciate Songaia giving me that chance and I don't need to do it again.

—Marilyn Hanna-Myrick

Move-in was a relatively orderly and joyous process. All but two of the households were able to move in by October and the remaining two moved in by November. An Open House and celebration was held in November with invited guests, including the various professionals who had worked with us, various county officials who had been particularly helpful, friends and colleagues.

CHAPTER THREE

Living Together in Community

Perhaps some of the most poignant challenges and greatest learnings in community happen in the realm of living together. This is where our lives come together and overlap on a daily basis. It is where our notions of privacy and personal boundaries are tested. It is where we experience the most profound demands on our abilities to work and interact with each other. It is also where we discover many of the joys and much of the creativity of living in community that make it so worthwhile.

Cooking and Eating Together

The heartbeat of Songaia takes place around community meals. This is a time when members can check with a gardening teammate as to whether the seeds have been ordered. It is when Songaians get to choose whom they would like to talk to over dinner. It is also where the kids and adults show up together in both creative and spontaneous ways. And, on Monday evening, before the meal, it is a time for Songaia to do what it loves to do even more than eating —we sing!

During the first months of living together we made a critical decision that has set the tone for our community eating patterns. Those of us who had been living together prior to construction knew that it was possible to eat most of our dinners together. The newly formed food committee, affectionately dubbed, the

Fabulous Food Folks (FFF), proposed to the whole community that we experiment for three months with five meals per week, four dinners and brunch on Saturday. Members agreed to pay for three months on an experimental basis. The FFF encouraged members not to concern themselves with fairness, but rather to focus on the value of the program. At the end of three months, the FFF asked, "Are you getting enough and are your food needs being met?"

Before two months had gone by, most of the fears about why the program wouldn't work had been addressed and there was a growing confidence that we could sustain it on an ongoing basis. That confidence was well-founded, as the food program continues basically as it was established. Every so often, someone raises an issue, and we go back to the question of "enough" and, or how can we make it work better for you? There were small problems but none that seemed insurmountable.

For a variety of reasons, most cohousing communities do not eat together as often as we do, varying from one to three meals per week, or as infrequently as once per month. Although these communities have fully equipped kitchens, there is reluctance to commit to the responsibility of purchasing and preparing for frequent meals. Some communities do not imagine a support structure that handles purchasing of foods, so therefore it becomes the responsibility of the cooks. Some communities rely on potlucks to bring them together.

Here is how it works at Songaia. On Saturday morning someone from the FFF posts a new sign-up sheet for meal preparation and clean up. Saturday morning, before or after breakfast, is often a good time for folks to choose which slot they want to take in the next two or three weeks. At any one time, there are three weeks of sign-up sheets posted. For the program to work, it requires that each person sign up for one slot per week, choosing from the two cooking and two clean up slots. The person who signs up for lead cook must submit their menu to the FFF by Thursday evening so the committee can do the inventory of the pantry and decide what has to be purchased on Friday morning.

Using Spirit When the System Gets Stuck

The food program relies on many people performing their particular roles in a timely fashion. Not having the menus turned in on time became a major obstacle to food purchasing, so Rachel, who was responsible for collecting menus, came up with a scheme of giving virtual prizes for the first cook to submit their menu. The virtual awards were announced to the whole community and became something we looked forward to because of the clever and often comical nature of the virtual awards, e.g., a virtual Taj Mahal, a virtual giant pumpkin pie, the virtual world's smallest violin. The strategy, which took place over many months, was quite effective in raising consciousness and shifting the pattern of cooks submitting their menus on time, or at least indicating when they will have their menus ready.

—Fred Lanphear

In 2000, when the food program was started, the cost was $80 per month per adult. As of 2010, the cost is $120 per month per adult, an increase of 50% over ten years. The cost for children is pro-rated until they are 16 years old, at which time they qualify as adults. This fee covers the five meals per week plus access to the pantry, where almost all "staples" can be found. The pantry is ample enough that families who can live without a lot of extras can easily eat deliciously and nutritiously on pantry food and common meals without having to go to the grocery store for food. The only other cost is a commitment to fill one slot per week, either cleaning or cooking.

Meal preparation and cleanup takes a team of four; a lead cook, a second cook—affectionately called the "second banana," a set-up person who also helps clean up, and a cleanup person. The set-up person is usually the first person on the scene. His or her job is to empty the three dishwashers and to set up the dining room. The cooks arrive around 4:00 pm. The lead cook is in charge and assigns the second banana his or her tasks. The meals generally consist of a main dish for carnivores and one for vegetarians, a vegetable dish, a grain or starch and a salad bar. The meal is laid out on a buffet table that can be accessed from two sides. Each dish is labeled to indicate the presence or absence of dietary restricted ingredients, e.g. dairy, soy, etc. After the meal is prepared and before the dinner bell is rung, the Second Banana fixes plates for any members who cannot attend the meal and have signed up to have plates saved for them.

After the meal the kids and adults take their dishes to one of the dishwashers, scrape and place them in the machine. The cleanup folks put the food away, wash the pots and pans, wipe the dining tables, sweep the floor, wipe down the kitchen counters and start the dishwashers. Some folk take this opportunity to take leftover food home with them for their next day's lunch.

Over the past eight years, there have been three families who have chosen to withdraw, either temporarily or indefinitely, from the full food program. For two of these families the decision was based on their own food restrictions and preferences. Another family found it difficult to cope with the lively energy of the dining room. One of these families pays a monthly fee to cover some pantry items they use, but does not show up at mealtime. Another family will often bring their prepared food to the dining room and eat with us. The other fixes her own food during pre-allergy season to build her immune system, but usually brings her food to the dining room and shares the community time with other residents.

Eating together has been very good for our community. It has provided a social setting for connection when people are generally enjoying themselves eating a good meal. It has brought members together in a close working situation for cooking or cleaning up. There has been general satisfaction with the quality of food, the savings in costs and human energy, and the awareness that it is moving towards ecological sustainability. The food program has been the most commonly told "success" story that members share when describing what it is like living in community.

Mealtime at Songaia

What's for dinner tonight? If I were cooking just for my family, it would probably be one of five or six somewhat boring but easy-to-make meals. Luckily for my family, we live at Songaia and dinner could be…well just about anything.

Curry chicken and tofu perhaps? That's likely to be a Sadhana or Nartano meal. Pad Thai? Well, that would be Fred, and we all look forward to those nights. African Ground Nut Stew? Stan makes this one. Salmon with capers? Could be Douglas or maybe Carol. If it is a burrito bar we know that Tom did the cooking. Or maybe tonight is spaghetti. That could be me, or any number of others. I have my favorites, of course, but I'm not really all that picky—almost every meal at Songaia is yummy.

Tonight is a Monday night, which means that we gather together and sing before the meal. I sit at a table with a few other adults, while my kids choose to sit with their friends. Craig is leading the singing tonight. We sing a couple old favorites with much enthusiasm, then one we don't know very well. Even though we have songbooks, the melody is off, but we mostly just laugh about it. People introduce guests next. There are a few tonight. Tom's parents are visiting and there is a woman who is interested in learning more about cohousing. Then Craig asks if there are any announcements. There are a few about various events happening around the community. By now, the cooks are ready to tell us about the meal. Susie is the lead cook and she has made a collection of dishes that, quite frankly, I have never heard of. One of them contains yucca.

But, I have learned that even if it looks a little weird, it is always a good idea to try Susie's meals. Susie is studying nutrition at nearby Bastyr University, and the meal turns out to be a yummy one.

The dining room is lively, with many discussions going on at once. We are talking politics at our table and at the next table over they are discussing something having to do with the chickens. The kids are having an animated discussion about their plans for a tree house. Monday nights tend to be a bit louder than the rest of the week, when the atmosphere tends to be more subdued. The energy on Mondays can be challenging and sometimes people (read children) need to be reminded to "use their inside voices," but in addition to the noise, there is also a feeling of warmth and welcome that more than makes up for a little chaos.

Often there are activities after Monday night dinner — birthday celebration, a circle, or a meeting. Those not called off to another activity frequently linger in the dining room chatting, sometimes helping with clean up. When I myself reluctantly get up to leave, I do so with a full tummy and a feeling of connection with my community.

—Rachel Lynette

Community Work

Working together as a community is an important part of life at Songaia. It became an aspect of our community culture during the development stage and has continued to be both a necessary and rewarding part of our lives. Following move-in after construction was complete, we continued working on "off-mortgage" projects. These were projects that we did as a community rather than including them as part of the construction costs: kitchen cupboards in the Common House, exit doors in the dining room, and French doors for the living room. In order to obtain an occupancy permit these projects needed to be finished quickly, as they impacted our use of the Common House. Workdays were orchestrated to accomplish these tasks. In order to get as many involved as possible, the project manager would list the tasks on the board after a meeting and ask folks to volunteer for the various tasks. Tasks generally included something for everyone, with folks preparing lunch, cleanup, painting, building, supplying childcare, etc.

A major project was to re-install our underground well-water system to the gardens and to each duplex. Since the well project required digging trenches to each duplex we decided to install an underground LAN system at the same time. We rented a trencher for a day and one team kept it going during the daylight hours and into the evening until it became impossible to see. After the trench was dug, another team came along and installed 1" PVC piping as well as risers with hose bibs. Another installed the conduit through which the internet cable was threaded as each length of conduit was connected. All was accomplished in one weekend, working two full days. This project contributed to long-term savings in the use of municipal water and internet access costs.

Another community project was to create a public plaza in front of the Common House. We had about $6,000 in the "Abundance Fund" that represented early development advances, donated to Songaia by former members. We announced a design workshop for all those who were interested in the project and seven came. We walked the area and began to imagine a circulation pattern focused on the front door. There were 4'x4' exposed aggregate slabs going from the front door stoop to our dining room. We decided to relocate them and create two approaches to the front door, one coming from the residences and the other from the guest parking area. This front entry became our Peace Garden, as it already had a Peace Pole from an earlier commissioning.

A landscape plan for the Peace Garden was designed and presented to the community along with a plan to use a portion of the existing "Abundance Fund." The project was approved

– on to implementation! A weekend was chosen in which we would have many strong people present since brute strength was needed. It was during the spring of the year when we would normally rent a tractor to rototill the garden, and since the tractor also has a front-end loader, we used it to move the slabs. The job was completed in the weekend we had the tractor, with only one toe smashed during the total endeavor. It was one of our more challenging projects, as it required a team effort to maneuver the huge slabs into place. There was a great sense of accomplishment when the task was completed.

We Can Do Just About Anything, Though Sometimes We Shouldn't

"I wonder if we could move these?" It seemed a simple question, and perfectly reasonable in light of the challenge to "totally redesign" the entrance to our Common House. But after the designs were drawn up, the workday scheduled, and the group of us gathered with wheelbarrows, shovels, pry-bars, and several lengths of metal pipe alongside the 6-foot square, 1500-pound slab of concrete, I wanted to say, "impossible."

By this point though, others in the group had found inspiration, had taken up the challenge. As we dug and lifted, levered and pried, I felt my sense of wonder begin to grow again. Perhaps we really could do this. And as the first of the 15 slabs of concrete began to move, I knew collectively we could do it.

"I wonder" becomes a much larger question in community, magnified by many hands, hearts and minds working together. When a common vision inspires us, it seems together we can do just about anything. Though sometimes, we shouldn't.

The large pine tree next to the common house was one of those times. It had grown too big and was now out of place in our peace garden. Yet it was so large and so close to the house, I wondered if we could safely bring it down. But once the inspiration took hold and someone grabbed a shovel to dig loose the roots, a common vision formed.

We encouraged and inspired each other: use the community truck to pull it away from the house and garden, keep the kids back, keep digging, chop the roots. As the rope strained and the tree began to give way, it seemed we had done it again. The tree didn't believe it. As a large root on one side gave way, the single rope from the truck couldn't control the fall. The tree shifted suddenly sideways, dropped across the garden and narrowly missed the house, snapping several large branches from a nearby sweet gum on its way down.

No one was hurt, the house was fine, and the peace garden has grown beautifully as a central gathering place for our community. A large, broken branch still hangs, high up in that tree. When the leaves are gone and I see that branch, I think about the power of community—the power of cultivating a common vision and a shared purpose with which a community can do wonders. I also recall why we should have professionals do some of it.

—Brian Bansenauer

The next phase of the project was brought on by the needs of the children. An old wooden jungle gym had been placed behind the Common House outside the playroom, because we thought this would be where the kids would choose to play. Wrong! The kids wanted to be where other folks congregated. So, it was decided to include the gym/swings in the plaza design. A team took on the task of adding an A-frame with three swings and a monkey bar to the gym set. The kids were so excited! The day the gym was moved and enlarged our 12 kids were all over it, swings, slide, monkey bars and all! It certainly is great to make decisions that work!

A final feature suggested to complete the plaza was a trellis and planter boxes that would provide soil for planting espaliered fruit trees and grape vines. This area in front of the barn had been a gravel parking lot, so without adding topsoil, plant growth was limited. The trellis would define an enclosure for the plaza and provide an attractive setting for the guest parking area. It also allowed for flowering plants to be grown in the planter boxes, which also served as a sitting bench.

After doing these types of post-construction projects for two to three years, we discovered that it was becoming more difficult to recruit folks for workdays. A shift was taking place in the community's readiness towards taking on projects. The Facilities Committee suggested a slow down on projects, partly because new projects tend to create future maintenance and partly because folks were tired of working every other weekend.

Although folks were getting burned out on big projects, there were still many upkeep and maintenance projects that had to get done. Unlike condominium associations and some cohousing communities that hire out most of their grounds and facilities maintenance, Songaia members see this as community work, an opportunity for being more self sufficient and sustainable. The Facilities team closely monitors the need for repairs and/or improvements. There are three to four on this team that divide the types of jobs among themselves based on their particular skill levels and passions. The jobs tend to sort themselves into carpentry, mechanical and electrical. Sometimes the jobs become more complex and a professional technician is called in, but in general, most jobs are handled by our own team.

An Electronic Safety Feature

As our woodshop became equipped with a table saw, drill press and chop saw, parents and others became concerned that our children would become fascinated and tempted to play with the power tools. An initial response was to lock the wood shop, but that was considered an inconve-

nience by those who use the shop. So Chuck, from our Facilities team, who happens to be an electronics engineer by training, designed and built a circuit control box that could be programmed to limit access to the power tools. Another small miracle is accomplished.

—Fred Lanphear

Another of area of work that requires continual expenditure of energy is maintaining our huge landscape. The primary task is mowing. There are two riding mowers that can be used for mowing the commons and area around the playground. The drain-field and orchard mowing is done with a brush mower. Mowing and caring for the community flower gardens is the responsibility of the Biogaians, but the actual work is done by others who have taken this on as a special passion.

Most of the community work does not have an assignment structure that assures it will get done. Instead, there is a "passion principle" that is the primary mode of encouraging folks to step up and take on the job(s) they most enjoy or for which they have a passion. No one keeps track of whether everyone is "doing their share." We give "raves" to individuals whenever they take on a task, often at dinner but certainly at the monthly House Meetings, where we make time for sharing "rants and raves." A cultural norm exists that expects everyone to pick up some tasks without trying to structure it. In general, this works!

Getting everyone involved on a community task is often seen as a great challenge and accomplishment. One example is when there is need to do a purge of all the junk that accumulates in our open barn. Songaia folk believe they have discovered a new physical law – community abhors empty space and will fill it with junk. For the last purge of the barn, notices were posted almost daily for a week before the workday, announcing the "great event" that folks would not want to miss. Our self-appointed cheerleader made announcements at meals and created such excitement around the event that folks were afraid if they were not there, they would certainly miss out on the fun. Sure enough, when the day came, a least one member from each family unit was available and the task was completed with gusto.

We're All in This Together!

I was asked by a member of the Navigators, the steering committee for the community, to lead a workshop in a House Meeting to address the issue of limited participation in taking responsibility for community tasks. This was about five years after move-in and there seemed to be inequities in how work was getting done or not being done. I don't know whether I was expected to place a "guilt-trip" on folks or embarrass them into taking on more responsibilities, but what I did was to ask each person to share the roles of care that they performed on an ongoing basis. It was awesome to discover things folks did "behind the scenes" that most did not know about. This included everything from changing light bulbs to breaking down cardboard boxes in the pantry. It was a spiritually uplifting event and indirectly accomplished its intent – to inspire folks to see themselves collectively responsible for doing the work of the community.

—Fred Lanphear

One community task that is done by assignment is cleaning the Common House. This had been attempted on an ad hoc basis by the Community Works Committee, but it was very difficult to get it done in a timely manner. Finally, the committee proposed that a team of two people would sign up each month to keep the Common House clean. The committee put together a weekly and monthly set of chores in a 3-ring binder that could be checked off as it was accomplished. Sign-up is at the beginning of the calendar year. A couple of individuals who were not fond of cleaning arranged to pay someone else to take their slot or traded some other favor, such as child care. Chris, a 10-year old, saw this as an opportunity for making some money that he could use to pay for piano lessons. He has become one of our best cleaners, and the most enthusiastic!

Doing the work of community is sometimes the source of great resentment. It raises the concern of inequity in regards to those who may not be doing their fair share. In general, Songaia has not focused on coercing or requiring participation, since we do not feel this is a long-term solution. Instead, we have worked at creating excitement and satisfaction around doing the work and connecting community members with the kinds of tasks they enjoy, or are willing to do. The notion that the community facilities and landscape are an extension of your home, particularly if tours come through frequently, helps to give members a greater sense of purpose for doing the work. Acknowledgement and expressions of gratitude also help.

Community Celebrations

Another critical pattern that underscores our life together in community is our celebrations. Next to mealtimes, no other type of activity receives more attention than do our times of celebration. We hold celebrations to honor individuals, to recognize the changing seasons, to honor our interdependence with each other and the earth, and to honor "Tradition."

Individual birthdays are honored in the month they occur, usually in groups of three or four people with birthdays in the same month. However, each person is individually honored by answering the birthday questions. These questions are:

- How many years are you celebrating, i.e., how old are you?
- What has been a significant event for you this year, or an image that holds what the year has been about for you?

• What is the challenge of the coming year, or what are you looking forward to?

• How can the community support you in the coming year?

After all the questions have been answered, the person asking the questions affirms the individual celebrating the birthday by sharing ways in which the person's presence and contributions to the community are acknowledged. After the "birthday questions," individual cakes or desserts with candles are brought to each person being honored. This is followed by singing of the birthday songs to all who are celebrating their birthdays and dessert for all. The birthday celebration has become a very meaningful occasion for both young and old. The children will sometimes participate in asking other children the questions and offer their affirmations. Knowing these questions are going to be asked provides an opportunity to be conscious of the significance of each year.

Orchestrating the Birthday Celebrations

What is your favorite dessert that you would like on your birthday? That is the question I asked each Songaian. The desserts chosen were as elegant as Baked Alaskan Pie and as earthy as Mud Cake with gelatin worms. Mud Cake was initially a favorite of many kids but soon became a favorite of some adults.

One of the exciting traditions at Songaia is the celebration of each person's birthday. I had the honor of serving as the Birthday Shaman for 5 years, a task I thoroughly enjoyed. My role was to provide what the birthday celebrant most wanted for a dessert and in most cases was able to provide it. On rare occasions the celebrant would leave the choice up to me or, also rarely, I would suggest a dessert to the celebrant.

Occasionally when a birthday celebrant requested a dessert they also requested a specific baker and when that occurred, I attempted to enlist that person's help. But more commonly, the selection of bakers fell to me and I chose one or more as needed. I usually baked one or more of the desserts myself and on rare occasions, did more. Maybe twice in my 5 years, I baked the entire suite of desserts because all the usual bakers were unavailable.

As Birthday Shaman I often chose the person to ask the birthday questions, but frequently I would ask the celebrant to choose whom they would like to ask the questions. I am very fond of the way we celebrate our Songaian birthdays and though I have retired from active duty, so to speak, I happily fill in as needed.

—Douglas Larson

One of the ways we celebrate whenever we come together is by community singing. If you were to stand outside the Common House on a Monday evening when we do our weekly community gathering, you might hear voices singing songs like "Simple Gifts" or "New Community Bound." Sometimes the songs are created by one of the members, like the following words sung to the old tune, "I love the Mountains":

I love Songaia, I love community,
I love the flowers, the dandelions, and the trees,
I love the people, they mean so very much to me,
Boom-de-ah-da, boom-de-ah-da, …

Solstice celebrations, especially Winter Solstice, is one that many look forward to, as it marks the turning point for the days to become longer and it allows for those who like to drum and dance, or otherwise express their enthusiasm, to become highly animated. It is a time to reconnect to the natural rhythms of our solar system and express joy and gratitude that, once again, the darkness will be turning to light. The drama is part of the ritual that comes from and honors the indigenous culture that once inhabited the land on which we live.

Other Earth-related celebrations that have become an important part of our culture are Festival of the Earth and Thanksgiving. The Festival of the Earth combines Earth Day and May Day dynamics as we usually include earth care activities, like tree planting, along with a May Pole dance. Thanksgiving is like a three-act drama: in the first act we do a ritual, like the Iroquois Thanksgiving Address; the second act is the feast; and the third act is a ritual of sharing what we are thankful for personally. This third act is done before we fill ourselves with pie and other desserts.

The Dance Goes On!

The logistics for doing our May Pole dance have become routine, as we have a permanent hole in the Commons to insert our pole in after we strip it of last year's weavings. Our ability to perform the dance that produces a finely woven pole does not seem to improve from year to year, but that does not dampen our enthusiasm or enjoyment of doing the dance. The challenge may be related to including small children and tall adults that tend to create frequent entanglements. One year the rain was too heavy to do the dance outdoors, so we decided to do it in the barn. Since we did not have a hole to put the pole in, Fred stood and held the pole upright while the rest of us danced around the pole and accomplished our usual entanglements. There is a consistency in our weaving pattern from year to year. At the top of the pole, there is no semblance of a weave pattern, but about a third of the way down the pole, the weave pattern begins and usually continues evenly until we finish at about waist height. What does change from year to year is the background music for the dance. When we first started doing the dance, we used taped music with amplification. We now bring in professional musicians who stay after our potluck dinner and perform for us as we set up the dining room for dancing. Last year we had a Blue Grass musical group called Squirrel Butter play for us.

—Fred Lanphear

During our extended development period, we noticed that our spirits lagged toward the end of summer. We decided that we need to go on a retreat where our full attention was focused on relaxation and having fun. We established an annual tradition of setting aside a weekend around Labor Day where we would find a campground or a site where we could set up tents, an outdoor kitchen, a shelter to get out of the sun or rain, and just enjoy each other. The highlight of the weekend is usually Saturday evening, when we sit around a campfire, sing songs, and create our yearly story by going round robin with each person, adding a word until everyone has contributed. The collective story is always an enjoyable activity and sometimes is remembered for its humor.

Some of the Kids' Favorite Celebrations

Scott, one of the adults, asked the group of young people, "What's your favorite celebration at Songaia and why is it your favorite?"

Without much time for thought, Natasha piped up with, "My favorite is May Day, May Day with the May Pole. I love dancing and I loved that chick who came to tap dance, sing and play violin."

"My favorite celebration," said Amelia, "is either Thanksgiving or New Year's. At Thanksgiving, we eat lots of yummy foods and hang out. At New Year's, we always jump on all the bubble wrap, and that's fun!"

"I really like Easter," remarked Lily. "I remember when I was like really little, and I just loved running around and finding eggs in the bushes and grass. One year, Chris and I found the same egg. Chris said he found it first and I said no that I did and I took it and ran away. It was fun to win a fight with Chris!"

Ian glanced around the informal circle and filled in, "I like either Thanksgiving or New Year's because at Thanksgiving, we always have that big party. And, we get to eat lots of good stuff like pecan pie. New Year's was neat because I got to taste some champagne and stomp on all that bubble wrap!"

*"My mom started that—the bubble wrap stomping," confessed Lucy.
"It's neat on New Year's Eve 'cuz we get to stay up until—like twelve
o'clock midnight or one o'clock in the morning," Chris added. "I'm all
for the bubble stomping, too, right at midnight!"*

*"I remember one year when I was about in the second grade, I think.
It was New Year's. And, while the adults were doing all that boring stuff,
toasting and talking about the next year, we kids went downstairs and
played 1985 about ten times as loud as the radio would go and rocked
out! Okay!" smiled Lucy.*

As some of us age, a higher priority has been placed on comfort and convenience. This past year we decided to stay at Songaia for the retreat, do fun activities, and go to a park with a
lake where we could do kayaking and swimming. We came back
to Songaia to do our traditional gathering around a campfire.
There was considerable resistance to do the retreat at Songaia, as
there was concern that folks would not detach themselves from
their computers, telephones and chores. This was not a problem,
as everyone tried to be engaged in the retreat.

Annual Retreats

*The Songaia Annual Retreat is a wonderful time to take the whole day
bonding with the community. Most folks show up to these, and it's a
different context in which to get to know each other.*

*At the retreats the emphasis is usually on playing games and having
fun. We have done a variety of things for retreats, including camping;
however, in recent years members have elected to stay on the property.
What I especially love about annual retreats is the opportunity to learn
about and get to know a different side of people than I usually do. At
the last retreat, through playing a game in which we guessed past facts
about each other, I learned a lot about various members' backgrounds,*

and it was stuff that I wouldn't have guessed or most likely found out about any other way.

I find the Annual Retreats important to our community culture. Retreats are always in the summer; they are geared toward relaxing and kicking back, and they provide a great contrast to our usual "work and get it done" ethic around here.

—Cyndi Kershner

The final celebration of the year takes place on New Year's Eve and the following day. This has been an annual tradition for over 15 years. There are components of the New Year's celebration that are included each year, although modified slightly. We begin with a celebrative dinner. Sometimes it has been potluck, but in recent years it has been an opportunity for one of our gourmet cooks to really get creative. After dinner, we see the annual Songaia slide show with a musical background, followed by creating our Wall of Wonder for the year we have just completed. Photos and Sticky Notes with events of the year written on them are posted on an 8' x 30" high poster board that remains on the wall in the dining room until the following New Year's celebration. We then reflect on what the year was about and come up with images that capture the spirit of the year. Other activities before midnight, at which time we toast in the New Year, include coming up with a theme for the coming year (e.g. Rejoice and Create in 2008), ceremonially burning the prayer flags from two years ago and circle dances. The next day starts with a late breakfast, creating prayer flags for the coming year, the annual gifts to the community, sharing individual intentions for the coming year and planting bulbs that were used in our Solstice celebration. The afternoon is movie time with folks seeing a video shown at our own Songaia Synema or going to a local cinema. The celebration ends with dinner out at a local Chinese restaurant.

Winter Solstice

Imagine looking up through the skylight into the darkness of the night! Only the stars light the winter solstice sky! As you look up, you see your own face in the skylight, now lit by the circle of candles below. Such a connection to the natural world! Winter Solstice is one of my favorite times here at Songaia. Although we sometimes have rain, we often have a clear dark night in which to celebrate the darkness and drum, dance and sing in the light!

We begin the evening by gathering in the living room of the Common House. You would hear the singing that accompanies most of our times together. This time it might be the song, "Darkness," and later in the evening, "The Light is Returning." Walking in silence with a single drum beat to the labyrinth softly glowing with small blue lights; circling the labyrinth, then following the pathway lit with luminaries and finding our way to the yurt. The circular shape of the yurt surrounds the circle we form with adults and older children. The younger children do their own darkness experience and then join us as we call in the light.

Winter Solstice is a time of reflecting, letting go of unnecessary baggage, looking forward to the return of the sun in the sky each day. It is a time of wild celebration and acknowledgment that the light WILL return in our lives and that it always has. Sharing our thoughts and hopes with our beloved community is such a gift — I would not trade my life here at Songaia for any other place on Earth. Winter Solstice is a time of waiting and of gratitude!

—Nancy Lanphear

Although our celebrations have an annual rhythm and repetitive quality, they seldom become boring. Creativity is injected into each activity as if it was the first time we were doing the event. The celebrants, with help from individuals with a passion for doing particular types of events, each year manage to maintain a seamless flow of celebrations that sustain the spirit life of the community.

Organizational Structure and Decision Making

Orchestrating our life together requires structure and intentionality. This has evolved mostly from the way we organized ourselves during development. We then adapted our structure to meet the requirements of our bylaws. Our overall legal structure is that of a condominium association with every member on the board of directors. This means that all of us are involved in the decisions that affect the life of the community. This may seem overly cumbersome but we have found ways to make many decisions relatively quickly and painlessly. In this way everyone in the community takes full ownership and responsibility for the community.

We developed a steering committee during the development phase called the Navigators. This structure continues to be the group that keeps in touch with the pulse of the community and orchestrates the monthly House Meetings and facilitates Sharing Circles. The House Meeting is designed to help us monitor and improve the practices of how we live together. The Sharing Circles provide us with the opportunity of sharing from the heart around topics of broad community interest. Members are encouraged to take their turn as a Navigator. When someone volunteers to be a "Navigator" it is for a three-year term. This results in a new mix of Navigators each year – some who have already served a year or two and some who are just beginning their terms. Usually, new folks join at the annual meeting in January to replace those who are retiring. The officers of the board are elected from among the Navigators.

Other committees that take responsibility for different aspects of community life are the following:

- **Fabulous Food Folks** – develop policy, plan and coordinate logistics for our food program.
- **Biogaians** – plan and coordinate care of the community gardens and landscape.
- **Celebrants** – plan, coordinate and find facilitators to orchestrate celebrations.
- **Community Works** – develops and oversees model for cleaning common facilities.
- **Community Relations** – encourages interaction with the neighborhood.
- **Facilities** – responsible for maintenance and development of physical facilities.
- **Finances** – responsible for bookkeeping, invoicing, taxes, payments and budget.

Each of these committees has both the responsibility and authority to operate with considerable freedom in carrying out their tasks. Most committees have budgets they manage without oversight.

There are no spiritual leaders, managers or titular leaders at Songaia. We practice collective leadership, in which different folks take charge of particular tasks or projects. The leadership is generally associated with the person who is most passionate about the work taking on the leadership in that arena of activity.

Decision-making has been an unfolding process at Songaia. Beginning in the development phase, as described in Chapter 2, Songaia has explored various techniques in facilitating the consensus process of making decisions. The values that were used in selecting the most appropriate form are inclusiveness, clarity, intentionality and simplicity. We continue to facilitate consensus decision-making at our house meetings, posting announcements of the meeting agenda at least five days preceding the meeting. As this process is seldom done quickly, we have used other approaches to allow us to make many decisions requiring community consent.

One of these approaches, the Decision Board, has been an extremely helpful tool in making most of our decisions. This requires that an individual or committee prepare a proposal and post it on the Decision Board in the Common House. At the time of posting, an announcement is sent out by email informing everyone that it has been posted. Along with the proposal, a consent sheet is posted for members to initial their consent, ask questions or indicate the need for discussion. If discussion is needed, a meeting(s) can be arranged after a community meal, where concerns can usually be addressed.

The Great Chicken Decision!

Larry and Kathleen had an ongoing interest in raising chickens. Whenever they broached the topic in casual conversation someone would invariably say they didn't want a rooster crowing in their backyard. They did not decide to pursue their original intent because Larry was not interested in raising chickens without a rooster. After five years had passed Kathleen said she still wanted to raise chickens, even if they could not have a rooster. So Fred and Cyndi joined Kathleen and put together a proposal with the following intents:

- *for the education of our children*
- *to fertilize and weed the garden*
- *to produce quality eggs for the community*

The proposal assured folks that there would be no rooster, there would be no accumulated smell since the chickens would be moving weekly, and that there was someone ready to take care of the chickens.

The two main concerns raised were:

- *One person had grown up in a village where chicken odor permeated the village and he did not want to create a similar situation at Songaia.*
- *Two persons expressed concern about the prospects of spreading Avian flu.*

After some discussion, the one person was assured that chicken odor would not be a problem with only 12 chickens and their continual moving across the garden. The Avian flu folks decided they could bracket their fears until there was an actual outbreak and then the chickens might need to go. The proposal was approved.

Post Script: When the first 12 sexed chicks were purchased and raised, it was noticed that one was developing a larger comb. Sure enough, one of the chickens was a rooster. The kids thought the rooster was quite handsome. They also knew he might be headed for the chopping block so they decide to name him "Dead Meat." However, there was no ground swell from the "rooster haters" to call for his execution. Perhaps, they were not ready to take on the kids' wrath. In fact, one of the dads, who had been one of the early skeptics for raising chickens, now became the champion for saving the rooster. The rooster was renamed Rudy and still lives happily among the hens today.

—Fred Lanphear

We discovered during the development process that making decisions by consensus in an open meeting was generally a formula for extended discussion that could lead to frustration and, often, no resolution. Until a group decides to work at consensus and moves through the propensity to talk every decision into the ground, the process can be challenging. This is related to one expression of diversity in a community. If you were to describe how the members of the community align themselves with ease of making decisions, you would find, on one extreme, those who are very loose about how specific decisions are made, and on the other extreme, those who are very specific, or require copious details, and a variety of perspectives. "Word-smithing," or the art of choosing just the "right words," often becomes a barrier to forming consensus. It is another reason the written proposals seem to flow more smoothly. If folks are blocked by choice of words, they can offer new wording to the person presenting the proposal and it can be changed.

Being able to come to consensus is not just about learning how to make agreements. It is about building trusting and supportive relationships. The foundational work of decision-making in community is in effective House Meetings and Sharing Circles, as well as all the other community activities that build intimacy and trust, in addition to forgiveness.

House Meetings are designed to celebrate our accomplishments, identify where we need improvement, and help forge a common mind around topics of mutual interest and concern. We seldom make decisions in House Meetings, although we will often identify areas where change or new decisions are needed. House Meetings open with singing, a roll call of each Unit, and some form of check-in, either in a round robin fashion or in dyads, triads, or larger sized group. "Rants and Raves" are a major focus of each House Meeting. Rants, issues or concerns, and Raves, affirmations and accomplishments, are our monthly accountability and celebration of life together. The rants, or issues, are not discussed during the meeting except to say who will take responsibility for its resolution. The House Meetings will generally focus on one or two topics, usually in the form of a report or workshop. House Meetings are often a time to gather input on a proposal that the Navigators or some other committee will be submitting to the Decision Board. This encourages broader participation in creating proposals while enticing others to follow through with the proposal. The meetings close with announcements and circling with a closing song.

A technique called Open Space was recently introduced into our House Meetings for discerning topics of emerging interest. This approach has been helpful in giving impetus and form to new initiatives. A recent Open Space workshop broke into three topics: one on community vehicles, one on lights in the living room, and another on engaging kids in setting up for dinners. A task force came out of the first, and actual implementation of suggested activities resulted from the other two groups. This technique has the value of mobilizing and giving form to existing passion.

Sharing Circles are also an important opportunity for listening to each other's perspectives and becoming aware and respectful of the diversity in the community. The intent of the circles is to choose a topic that has some interest to almost everyone in the community and create a dialogue process that allows all to participate. In 2007 we focused on reviewing our seven values, taking one per circle and brainstorming where we were making progress achieving our values and where we need to do more work and what that looks like.

A recent circle visited the topic of recovering the spirit around community work projects. The discussion indicated there would be support for projects but not commitment from everyone to do the physical work to make them happen. Folks were becoming more selective of how they would allocate their energy to ongoing work in contrast to new projects. This was not a surprise, since it reflected what was already taking place. It did allow us to accept the fact that everyone does not need to participate in every project. It was also a reminder that any new project needs to have a sufficient number of people who have the passion to make it happen.

Learning to Manage Our Finances

The first three to four years were the most difficult for making decisions about how much money was needed to operate the community. We had limited historical data on which to base our projections. Also, since we were still focused on completing old and new projects, we tended to project higher budgets and would find ourselves with a surplus at the end of the year. The question we faced in the next year was whether to roll the surplus into lowering next year's cost or maintaining the surplus to complete the projects. We chose the latter option in the early years. After repeating this pattern for two to three years, it was agreed to not budget money for projects until the energy was available to do them. Budgeting was difficult and time-consuming in those early years. For the last three years, budgets have been approved with relative ease.

There are two bookkeepers and one other member who make up the Finance Committee. The bookkeepers send out invoices to each family every month with their monthly costs. The invoice is a composite of each family's monthly assessment, their food program costs, any donations they have committed to in support of projects, personal use of the community truck and any purchases from the Community Exchange or from the wholesale distributor.

The Community Exchange is non-food items, such as toilet paper, cleaning materials, etc., that is purchased wholesale and made available at cost to the members. These items are kept in the community pantry on shelves with a monthly tally sheet for each family to record items as they take them. This ensures getting environmentally sensitive products at the lowest cost possible. Families can also order items such as toothpaste and other hygiene products from the wholesaler by making their needs known the week before the order goes in. If a community expense is incurred by a member, this is paid back at the end of each month.

The monthly assessment consists of a variety of annual operational costs and longer-term replacement reserve funds. These costs are mostly allocated to each unit based on the size of the unit, but some are prorated based on the number of adults living in the unit.

The Abundance Fund originally held monies from donations of previous members. As those funds were utilized or designated for projects, some members proposed maintaining this fund so there would always be funds available. Members were invited to make monthly pledges into the fund. Only four families contribute in this way. Consequently, when projects are proposed, they usually specify so much from the Abundance Fund and the remainder from individual donations. Those who have contributed to the Abundance Fund may decide that their contribution is included in funds drawn from the fund, or may choose to contribute more. Others decide on a project by project basis how much, if any, they will contribute. A suggested amount may be included in the proposal.

Financial matters have seldom been a major issue. There have been questions of fairness raised in certain situations but have usually been resolved by adjusting fees one way or another.

Operating from Abundance

During the initial years of budgeting, it was frustrating to budget for "the extras"—special projects such as adding trellises, buying more trees, upgrading our guest rooms, electrifying outbuildings, etc. Doing this on an annual basis inevitably meant that projects would get informally proposed and then wait for months until the budgeting cycle came around. Then they would go through a prioritization process in which various projects competed for the limited, indeterminate amount of funds that we could approve as a group—this meant that all of the "pet projects" proposed by various members and committees required everyone to compare and contrast the projects and decide which would be funded.

The process was excruciating. One improvement was to approve the operating and reserve budgets separately from the project budget. Another frustration was that some of the funded projects no longer seemed to be of interest to the person that had proposed it many months earlier. Some projects became running jokes as they were placed into the annual budgeting cycle year after year with no progress in making them happen.

By running projects through our conventional budgeting, all unit owners pay about the same amount for every project. This meant that families that were the most concerned about their expenses would carefully watch the size of their monthly assessments. They tended to avoid any "extra costs." Those with fewer financial limitations—or who placed higher value on "communal" enterprise—would become quite frustrated that we couldn't agree to fund some projects they viewed as inexpensive, especially when split 13 ways.

Over the first few years of our life together, it became clear that some Songaia members would support almost anything, while others objected to most projects that involved added expense to them. I began to wonder whether everyone needed to pay the same for every project. One concern was how differential payments might affect feelings about power and influence... those with more means or willingness to spend might "vote with their dollars" in ways unavailable to others.

I proposed creating an anonymous fund for year-round ad hoc project budgeting. Members could contribute to the fund anonymously, either on a recurring basis (annually or monthly), or on a one-time basis. Those that wanted to help things happen, with less regard for costs, could choose to tax themselves to grow the fund. We already had an Abundance Fund that was created when some of our early members decided that they didn't want all of their early investments refunded. It was proposed to use this fund for the anonymous contributions as well.

My theory was that the new process for project funding would be that any member or committee would write up a project proposal with a budget that could draw on some or all of the funds from the Abundance Fund. The proposal could call for additional, earmarked anonymous payments.

Over time, fewer people have contributed to the Abundance Fund using recurring payments. The fund continues to grow slowly and has never come close to being depleted. This approach has not really solved the issue around funded projects that are not actually completed. The Abundance Fund now has earmarked money waiting for a variety of funded projects to actually begin. However, those projects *are now more visible and it may slow down folks who would other-wise propose a bunch of new projects while their previously funded projects are still waiting for action.*

Since this plan was put in place, we have not had any proposals denied because of financial constraints. Another important outcome of this approach is that our annual operating and reserve budgets are MUCH easier to agree on, as almost everybody accepts that we are really doing our best to keep those budgets to the minimum level required to prudently fund our organization's ongoing financial needs.

—Craig Ragland

CHAPTER FOUR

Relationships in Community

We respect and celebrate the variety of cultures and backgrounds of the people who live in this community, and those who may come in the future. In all facets of community life, we strive to incorporate this variety, experimenting with different foods, exploring new approaches to living, and creating rituals that draw on other walks of life. We honor people for who they are; we encourage and welcome diversity.

—Songaia Value Statement, "Open to Diversity"

Diversity is frequently thought of in terms of racial, religious, sexual preference and national differences. We have no racial differences, some religious and sexual preference differences, and one member who is an extra-national. Yet, we experience our diversity every day. It shows up in our many relationships in all facets of our community life. It is at the heart of what makes a community thrive, co-exist, or fail. It is continually flowing and evolving. This chapter will strive to capture the types of relationships at Songaia, how they play out, where they flourish and where they get stuck.

It Takes a Village to Raise a Child

As a multi-generational community we are committed to investing in caring for and nurturing the children. This is obviously a very high priority for parents and it is a value that is supported by others. It is also one of the most challenging endeavors the community has encountered in living together. Defining common parameters for childhood behavior and expectations of parenting norms has generally been unattainable. However, we continue to strive for practices that work for most, do not offend others, and still enable the children to thrive.

Adults and children interact together on a daily basis at community meals. In the early years of eating together many of the children were quite young and sat with their parents. This allowed for a relatively calm and orderly mealtime atmosphere. However, there has always been an attraction for a "kids only" table and this is generally supported, unless it becomes too noisy, and then they are separated. As the children have grown older, they usually discipline themselves, knowing that the pattern of separation is a consequence. In the summertime, the children's table often shifts to the picnic table outside the dining room where they are able to express themselves more openly. They occasionally remind us adults if we are too noisy.

It Takes a Village to Raise a Child

It Takes a Village to Raise a Child. This is a phrase that has become almost a cliché…unless you live in community! The "village" of Songaia has been irreplaceable in my child's life. For ecological reasons, my husband and I decided to have one child. As an only child in community, she has been surrounded by "siblings" who continue to help teach her the lessons of sharing, compassion, getting along, teamwork and the joys of being with others. The adults have mentored her. It's not uncommon for an adult to be working on a project…and my daughter will come along to ask a million questions. In doing so, she has learned about topics I could never teach her: car engine workings, electrical circuitry, website design, starting plants from hardwood cutting, goat/chicken husbandry…and the list goes on.

As working parents, we have needed a lot of help with childcare over the years. We have swapped with other families that have children... and adopted elder members as grandparents. At common meals, my daughter gets to eat food I'd never cook at home like beets and brussel sprouts, which she learned she loves! Parenting in community is also amazing. I've always had support and advice for every challenging moment I've encountered. To raise a child in our world who becomes an engaged, self-assured problem solver while continuing to nurture one's own physical/emotional/spiritual journey as a parent...it takes a village...or at least a close knit community like Songaia!

—Michelle Grandy

My son Lucas has a chronic medical condition that has made it very hard for my husband and I to get away for even short amounts of time. One of our residents, Carol, is a nurse and also someone who devotes a lot of time to helping others in the community. She volunteered several years ago to watch Lucas for a weekend in order to give us time off from our caregiving duties. Since she was a nurse we had confidence in her to be able to do this, as it involved administering medicines and preparing special foods. Since she volunteered to do this she has taken Lucas for the weekend many times, and it has been so helpful in helping us to nurture our marriage so we could take the best possible care of our son. If we didn't live at Songaia, where there is definitely the village ethic toward raising kids, we would never have been able to get that need met.

—Cyndi Kershner

On Monday nights, when we sing before dinner, the children are present and usually join in the singing without prodding. On occasion, a child may be asked to choose the songs. When this happens we sing more of the "fun" songs, often experienced as "gruesome" to some adults, as illustrated in the following verse from "The Cat Came Back":

The man around the corner said he'd shoot the cat on sight.
He loaded up his shotgun full of nails and dynamite.
He waited in the garden 'til that cat came walking 'round.
Seven little pieces of the man was all they found.

In addition to the expectation of sitting and eating quietly, or at least not noisily, the children, like everyone else, are expected to clear their own dishes and put them in the dishwasher.

Children are encouraged to participate in as many community activities as possible. In addition to being recipients in the meal times, they are encouraged to help in the preparation and clean up. This happens most effectively when the parents provide appropriate encouragement. When a child does help out they are recognized with applause during the introduction of the meal.

The activities that are most successful in engaging children are the various celebrations. An annual talent show provides a grand opportunity for every child to perform, and they usually do. Halloween is another occasion in which there is total participation by the children. Other events, like solstice celebrations, will have some but not all children participating, particularly if their parents attend.

Occasionally the children will come up with a project they want to do. An adult may work with them to help them prepare a proposal that will be posted on the decision board, but children have also written proposals by themselves. This is usually a great opportunity for interacting with adults and encountering expectations that frequently are quite different from theirs. Even if the proposal is approved, the implementation of what seemed like a good idea may not happen. On proposals that are prepared in concert with adults, the adult will generally help make it happen. An example of this was painting the children's playroom and doing one wall as a mural.

Mentoring Program

One effort to increase adult–child interactions was the creation of a mentoring program. Some adults met to discuss how to connect the children who were 10 years or older to adults that were willing to serve as mentors. When the adults presented the idea to the children the response from each child was to name the person they wanted to be their mentor. It was fortunate in the early stages that there was not competition for particular adults. As the program evolved, certain adults became more in demand due to the attention they were known to provide. Initially, four children were each paired with a different adult of the same sex. Later configurations had mixed pairings.

There was no prescribed program. Each pair worked out their own schedule and type of activities. Pairings frequently took place around a common interest, such as computer games, gardening or creative expression. In other cases, a previous connection was the attraction that then became more structured. Pairs engaged in activities like computer games, bowling, making things together, going out to eat, attending events, and many others. Sometimes pairs worked together on community workdays. The conversations and mutual effort to create a working relationship were important outcomes in this structure.

Intergenerational encounters and ongoing relationships are not always easy, even in familial settings. The results of the mentorship experiences were mixed. Along with the good experiences there were the disappointments of unrealized expectations of both adults and youth. As in some family settings, there was the sense of guilt on the part of adults who felt they should be doing more or that they could be more effective. The overarching experience was a camaraderie built on a mutual trust of good intentions and respect for each other. While many pairings last for six months, or perhaps a year, the program has been through at least three different pairings that lasted for three to four years.

Mentoring Christopher

Last year they picked up the mentoring program again, so each of the kids who were nine or 10 and older could have a mentor for a year. I was really thrilled that Christopher picked me. I don't know how much we've actually done. Seems like we were doing more before I was his mentor. Lately we've done a few things. But it felt really special to be picked. We had an evening where we picked the people and the mentors and the kids got together and made little symbols out of Fimo clay? So Christopher and I made a chocolate chip cookie out of this Fimo dough, and then he cut it in half. Then we made little holes so after it was baked we could string it. So we each have half of a chocolate chip cookie on a shoestring to wear as our symbol of our mentor relationship. We've actually baked cookies a few times. We're also out there discussing our poor little garden plots during the summer.

I took him running the other night. He had a birthday just recently and he talked about running a six-minute mile. He asked if I'd take him running. Before we went out, I said, "well, I run really slow. I mean really slow." So we go out running and at some point he looks back at me, and he goes, "I had no idea what you meant by 'slow.'" I was like "Yeah, yeah." He'd run out ahead of me and then most of the time he'd wait. And I'd try to get him to run ahead and then run all the way back. But mostly he'd go forward and then stop and wait for me. We went three or four miles.

We now have added throwing Frisbee to the list of activities!

—Kate Aarden

Peer Relations

The relationships between children in the community is very familial and, generally, quite supportive. Children relate to each other as cousins or siblings. This exists as strong loyalties among the children, even though tensions develop. Pairings occur regularly and at other times groups of three or more is the norm. They are not always in the same configuration, although consistent patterns do exist over extended periods of time. Some pairings or groupings seem to be based on gender or follow the developmental cycles of the children, others are more inter-age and inter-gender.

Lucy's "Big Sister"

My daughter, Lucy, has enjoyed positive relationships with all of Songaia's children; however, I would point to her relationship with Alaina as being one of the more important relationships of her young life. Alaina and Lucy are five years apart. Lucy was just four years old when we moved to Songaia. In the early years, I sometimes worried about the friendship, as Lucy, being younger, was sometimes excluded from the older kid's activities. Alaina, like all adolescents, had some difficult times and could be moody and unkind. However, at some point in her teen years, Alaina emerged into one of the kindest young people that I know. At meal times she could frequently be found giving hugs to other community members, offering encouragement, or just emanating her contagious, cheerful enthusiasm for whatever was going on at the time.

Throughout the years, Lucy and Alaina have spent a great deal of time together. We love having Alaina along on family outings and they frequently spend nights together. I believe the two are more like sisters than friends. However, what I am most happy about is the positive effect that I feel Alaina has had on my daughter. Lucy has excellent social skills, and a tendency to be kind to everyone. This has lead to her making a lot of friends at her new Junior High and having a positive Junior High experience, something I do not take for granted. She usually copes well with conflict and can often defuse a stressful situation. I believe that she learned much of this from spending time with Alaina, who regularly models all of these skills. Now

13 and 18, the girls are still close, and I often find myself wondering if Alaina will always be a part of Lucy's life.

—Rachel Lynette

The "sibling" relationships that develop among the children are generally encouraged and supported by the parents. Families frequently include their children's friends in family outings as well as welcoming them into their homes.

The groupings at mealtime become more gregarious and frequently include all the younger children. The teens are more likely to congregate by themselves and sometimes they will choose to eat by themselves. The other place where there is more fluidity between children and age groups is at the playground. Children of all ages congregate and share the swings and jungle gym. The same is true in the playroom, although the teens are more likely to come together in the living room. Fort Can-be is the other place where the children, including the teens, may show up all together, particularly in springtime.

It has been exciting to watch how visiting grandchildren are assimilated into the mix of children. They are generally welcomed and seem to get special attention that elicits a desire among these children to want to return to Songaia. Their welcome does not seem to diminish with repeated visits. This seems related to Songaia children always wishing there were more children at Songaia. Occasionally, a younger child may be excluded by the older children because they are not able to fit in, but that is the exception and not the rule.

Healing Friendship

Soon after we moved into Songaia, my son Lucas developed a serious chronic illness. Previous to this, although having food allergies, he had been a typical kid and was part of the tribe of kids who roamed the property, playing for hours without much adult supervision. We called them our free-range children. Lucas was very happy as part of the tribe, often taking the role of leader among the younger kids, and also being one of the kids who got along with everyone most of the time.

After developing his illness, Lucas was largely housebound for about eight months. He was no longer able to participate in community events, and in the beginning felt isolated and depressed. After some time had passed, Christopher, one of the community's children, began a regular ritual of visiting Lucas. He would come over every day at the same time, and patiently do whatever my son could do that day. Since he lived about 100 yards from us, it was always very convenient for him to come over, which we were so grateful for. Christopher never got bored with Lucas, even when it was a sunny day and he would rather have been outside playing with the other children. He always encouraged Lucas and tried to cheer him up. Every day Lucas looked forward to the time when his friend would come over to visit; he would schedule his whole day around it, and his face would just light up when Christopher would walk through the door. His friend never failed to make him laugh and cheer him up, even if he was in pain and feeling lousy.

That December Lucas was able to get out for a while, and I took both boys to the store. To my surprise, they took turns conspiring how to buy Christmas gifts for each other with what little money they had. They were so excited to try to find things the other one would like. It felt like a modern version of "The Gift of the Magi," with both of them counting up their pennies to buy the other the nicest gift.

In remembering friends and acquaintances from my growing up, I honestly don't remember, at 10 and 12 years old, any friendships nearly this deep or meaningful. These kids are truly devoted to each other, having fun, looking out for each other's well-being, and growing up together.

I am so grateful that in the midst of a very difficult and trying time in his life and our life together as a family, that Lucas has had his friend to be there for him and help him through this. There is no way my husband and I would have been able to help Lucas feel valued and somewhat normal in the way his friend has been able to do for him.

Even though he has a chronic illness, he is still emotionally a normally developing pre-teen who needs the approval of his peers, and he has gotten this from his friend.

I shudder to think of being isolated in a typical suburban housing situation where neighbors really do not know or interact with each other, and my son having to go through this alone. In our community when the adults go through illnesses we often hold healing circles, where we express our caring and concern for the one going through the illness. There is an ethic of mutual concern promoted at Songaia, and all of us, adults and children alike, realize that we are interdependent and connected. I believe that this ethic filters down to the kids. They are not always angels, and they fight and get in trouble just like kids raised outside community. However, I think Christopher, being raised in this community ethic of interdependence, found it natural to love and care for his friend when he needed it most.

—Cyndi Kershner

Developmental Journey and Rites of Passage

Watching the children grow and develop is one of the great pleasures we as adults experience at Songaia. Even those of us who are not parents feel a sense of connection and pride in each child. Seeing the infants develop their personalities provides great joy and surprise. Even more dramatic is the journey of children becoming adolescents. Encounters during this transitional time are less predictable and sometimes frustrating. Greeting them may or may not elicit a response, depending on their mood or state of awareness. At other times, hugs may be the primary mode of expression, often coming in the form of an enthusiastic "group hug."

The community can play a helpful role during this transition from innocence and exploration to becoming a socially functional self among peers. This transition, for some (myself included), is one of the most difficult and perhaps traumatic times in our lives. There are sexually related biological changes taking place as well emotional and social changes. Community acknowledgement and support during this transition can be very helpful.

The women of Songaia have taken responsibility for creating a ritual that acknowledges the passage of Songaia girls into a stage of puberty marked by their first menses. The ritual marks the passage into a stage of sexual maturity that provides a new connection to the women of the community. It has become a simple ceremony of recognition and honor that the girls look forward to and deeply appreciate.

Young Womens' Coming of Age Ceremony

As the women of Songaia, we felt it important to celebrate the coming of age of our young women at the time of menarche. As our young women entered this important phase of life, we wanted them to feel celebrated, important, honored and embraced by the adult community of women. To this end, we met with our young women to design a ritual that would recognize the tender moments of childhood and symbolize this transition towards womanhood.

In preparation for the ritual, the young woman participates in the design of the ritual guided by a small group of women. A date is set. All the women of the community are invited as well as any other women who are important to the participant (grandmothers, aunts, adult friends). The young women of the community who have previously completed this ritual are invited, along with the girl we think is likely to experience menarche next.

The ritual has three important parts: 1) recognizing important parts of childhood; 2) symbolic crossing over to young womanhood; 3) gifts of sharing wisdom and welcoming into the community of women. The ritual has had a profound effect on young and old alike. I've been brought to tears at each ritual—so proud that our young women are strong in spirit. For some, that recognition has built their self esteem. For others, it is a way of staking claim to their young adulthood. For all, it is a bonding experience as we feel, as a community of women, a sense of responsibility in the raising of all the girls—of working together to guide them along the path to womanhood.

—Michelle Grandy

The psychosocial change that takes place during the teen years provides an opportunity for a rite of passage that is more extensive and applicable to both boys and girls. Songaia hosts a program that conducts rites of passage in which our children are encouraged and supported to participate. The rite of passage at this time is referred to as "Coming of Age," and is a three-week wilderness trek with a solo vigil and a re-entry ritual that acknowledges that the children have made a transition from childhood to becoming a youth. Others have chosen a church related program that holds similar values and rituals.

Embracing Diversity in Our Relationships

One of our greatest community assets is the diversity of skills and personalities that are present in the community. There are many career skills, such as architectural design, computer technology, nursing, midwifery, electronics, library science, etc., but perhaps more useful from a community perspective are the avocational skills, such as carpentry, electrical, mechanical, cooking, organization, facilitation, writing, music, gardening, designing, etc., that contribute to the collective skill set of the community. When these various skills are put to use, community creativity abounds.

There are as many personalities as there are individuals in the community. Each contributes to the richness of the social fabric. From the expressive to the introvert, the emotional to the rational, the wide range of personalities allows a creative and comprehensive approach to planning community activities and solving community issues.

Blending or integrating the various skills that come with the personalities into a good fit with community needs requires sensitive orchestration and multiple efforts. We have discovered that some personalities choose to work alone and do not fit into a workday pattern. Others want to work as a team but are challenged by the need that some individuals have to direct the activities. What has worked well is for individuals to sign up for the task(s) they prefer. This tends to result in groups that work well together. Sign-ups usually happen Saturday morning on a community workday. The person in charge of rallying the troops lists the different roles or tasks on the white board and asks for volunteers to assign themselves. The other approach is to post the list on a bulletin board over a period of days.

Beyond workdays, there are multiple opportunities for engagement. Creative dialogue and interaction often take place in committees or task forces, cooking or cleaning up after meals, or working together on a project. It is in these settings, over time, that community members come to know each other's patterns and propensities. This is where levels of trust are established. By trust, I mean: what can I realistically expect of the other based on what I know about him/her? It does not mean that I can expect the other person to meet MY expectations in terms of completion or timeline.

Laundry Fairies: Mystical Creatures Discovered in Community

I don't know about where you live, but here at Songaia we have laundry fairies. We have a laundry room that has three washers and three dryers. Only three out of 13 units have their own washer and dryer, so the laundry room is shared by many of us. In the laundry room we can literally interact with our neighbors' clean and "dirty laundry." It is one of many sacred places that can encourage us on our spiritual paths if we let it. It is a place where we can be asked to walk our talk of co-operation, consideration, patience and responsibility. We get to observe that some of us are not that interested in keeping track of clothes, time, shoes, etc., as others. It is here that we cannot deny that even though "we are all one" we have a great diversity of habits and ideas about order and other things.

Every once in a while, I will rush in to move my forgotten laundry so it is not in the way of the next person signed up. Sometimes I am in a harried state and feeling overwhelmed. Once in a while I will find my laundry neatly folded on the laundry table. It's my turn to try and guess who the laundry fairy is. There is usually one among us that volunteers to launder the Common House towels, washcloths and table clothes. I have heard stories of a laundry fairy who helps out by nicely folding these items and even putting them back upstairs in the Common House in their proper place before the regular person who does this job returns to do it. I have also seen a newly laundered load placed upstairs in the cafe area with a note that says: "Dear Laundry Fairies, if you have time please fold these. Thank you very much." I have talked about the laundry fairy with my son, when he started to use the laundry room. I have read emails out to the group that say, thank you to the laundry fairy who folded my stuff yesterday. Yes, the laundry fairy is alive and well at Songaia. Do you have any living near you?

—Barb Bansenauer

Member's intents toward the community are generally revealed by their presence in house meetings and sharing circles, often articulating their relationship to the community in these gatherings. Individuals are continually juggling their priorities and other commitments. Occasionally members overcommit themselves and are not able to follow through on their "promises." This leads to resentment and disappointment. These shortcomings are often accepted or forgiven if the person is perceived to have truly intended to carry out the task. If a pattern of not following through persists, the person's credibility and intentions are in question. One helpful way I find to understand where others are coming from is to believe the statement, "they are doing the best they can."

Extending My Comfort Zone

There are a lot of skills I don't have, but there are skills I do have. With cohousing, you have the opportunity to share your skills, share your gifts with other people. Before we moved in we were working on the second story of the barn that we were renovating for storage spaces for each unit. My whole family was here along with many other families for a workday.

I would have never tried this on my own, but we had Tom, an architect, and Larry, a carpenter and civil engineer, to lead us. And so we would do a lot of the labor and do things we would never try on our own, and they could lead the way, direct us and give us advice. And I could learn from them as well. That weekend we completed the whole second story loft floor, in a very short time. What I really enjoyed about doing this and was really hoping to see a lot of in cohousing—and I've seen it—is the opportunity to try things you would never dare try doing on your own because you don't have anyone to help guide you, or mentor you or make sure you don't "blow it," which can happen when you are on your own. So what I was really excited about in cohousing that I've been able to do is extend my comfort zone, try things I wouldn't try otherwise.

—James Olson

Honoring and Nurturing Gender Relations

Soon after move-in, there was energy to create separate gatherings of men and women. There was a general recognition that each gender had particular needs that could be met through gender circles that might not be met in gatherings of the total community. So, monthly men and women's circles were established. The women's circles have continued consistently while the men's circles have been more sporadic and at times non-existent. The meeting pattern either reflects a greater need among the women for the circles or their greater ability to organize and take responsibility for keeping the circles alive, or both.

The Men's Circle, in the formative stage, took the opportunity to individually share their life's journey and what they were looking for in community. Later circles were around barbershop quartet singing, going to a movie followed by gathering at a local pub, drumming circle, etc. The women's circles were frequently based on listening to and supporting each other, but also included songs, poetry, and occasional crafts projects.

In addition to monthly circles, the men and women schedule annual retreats. The retreats usually take place over a weekend and involves traveling to a campground or retreat center with cabins or similar accommodations. The retreats might have a theme around visioning men's or women's activities in the community, sharing vocational challenges and visions, cycles of life, etc. The men would use these opportunities to schedule side trips to see or do things of interest. Meal times and conversations are special for both men and women.

Multi-generational Sharing

We have a healthy mix of three generations: 10 children, 15 that are in midlife – between 30 and 50 years old, and nine that are over 60. Strong relationships have developed within and between these three age groupings that I will call children, adults and seniors. It is of interest that the strongest relations are not necessarily within groups but seem to be between them.

There are various affinities that form the basis for these relationships. These include intellectual and spiritual interests, common mission and/or organizational interests, lifestyle and/or family-like connections. Shared activities and resources include going on outings, common study, sharing vehicles and childcare.

Encountering Alaina

I don't know that I'd even moved here yet, but I came up for dinner one evening, and Alaina came over, she was just thrilled about my whole existence—that I was there. We had this instant rapport and it was so exciting to me. It was over a year ago and Alaina was approaching her sixteenth birthday. She sat with me and was totally engaged. She told me a whole bunch of jokes, and then I told her a couple of jokes (I have so few in my repertoire). After that evening, when I'd come by for visits, she would always give me a hug. She was just always thrilled to see me and I just don't know if I had words to express how that felt to me. It was very, very special, and exciting and really thrilling to be welcomed by this teenage girl and her enthusiasm, this extension of friendship just like that. It was lovely and continues to be lovely and loving.

—Kate Arden

Intentional and Spontaneous Gatherings Among Members

There are a variety of circumstances that bring together individuals or families from the community. Sharing a duplex provides opportunities to come together, perhaps to discuss landscaping, use of common porch area, or arrangements for pet care while a family is away. Other individuals or families come together because of common interests or needs. Some individuals and families like to go out to eat together. This frequently happens after a community Sharing Circle.

Some individuals or families connect to share resources or services. This includes ride or vehicle sharing, childcare, trips to the airport, household repairs, haircuts, etc. Special needs can be met when families are away on trips, such as mail pickup, pet care and plant watering.

When children or adults are involved in public performances, invitations are sent to the community, providing opportunities for community members to be supportive and connected with each other. There is generally good participation in these events by other members of the community, not just a token response.

Spontaneous conversations on the pathway are the norm when walking to the Common House, the laundry or to the parking lots. They can also happen on decks and patios when someone walks by and is invited to join in.

Acknowledging and Celebrating
New Relationships

Songaia has been blessed with the addition of new members via marriage and a new partnership. In a small community like ours, a new member can have a significant impact. Not only does a new member fill a gap in a family unit, he or she also adds new energy into the community.

When Nartano and Sadhana were married, their new relationship to each other and to the community was symbolized by holding the wedding and reception at Songaia. Brent's partnership relationship with Dorothy was informal, so we had a welcoming circle for him in which he was accepted as a full member. There was no orientation for either Nartano or Brent, as the community assumed that Sadhana and Dorothy would take the primary role in helping their new partners get acclimated to the community.

One could assume that living in community would limit your options of finding a partner. One of our earlier members chose not to purchase a unit and discontinued his membership fearing that living in community would hamper his chances of finding a partner. It is true that finding a partner that is also looking to live in community narrows the field, but it also acts as a filter in helping to select a mate who is compatible with the value of community.

Intern Wins Dorothy Prize for Excellence in Gardening

I had been a volunteer with Rite of Passage Journeys working with Stan Crow. I had retired early and wanted to find some meaningful volunteer work that I could do. I would come out and work for a day, eat in the dining room, stay overnight at the Crows' and put in another day before going home. I started to meet folks, talk with them and the next thing I know, Nancy proposed that I become an intern and work in the garden. The community would feed me and I could bring and stay in my little motor home and work through the summer. Then in September I would leave and continue on with my life, or at least that was the intent.

And so I started in mid-April. About the time I came, Dorothy had just had surgery on her foot and was in a wheelchair. I often would push her in her wheelchair to the Common House and back and in this way I got to know her. I like to watch a lot of movies but my DVD player died. I needed a place to watch movies, so I said to Dorothy, "Do you like movies?" So I started watching movies at her place. I would push her in her wheelchair and she would let me watch movies, and then I would go to my motor home. I had been divorced for a couple of years. I had taken a vow of poverty and a vow of celibacy because I didn't want to complicate my life. I was disabled and going through the steps of getting Social Security Disability. I was penniless, kind of living my life and trying to be useful. That was why I was interested in being a volunteer and doing something useful. So the garden was a challenge.

Suddenly, watching movies and visiting with Dorothy started to seem like it was maybe more, like dating, and that sort of frightened me. Not exactly frightened me but concerned me because that could lead to breaking my vow of celibacy, and I was pretty committed to leading an uncomplicated life. I was sort of working on re-establishing a relationship in my semi-usefulness with my children and my first wife was the vehicle for me to be in touch with my children. I talked with her often, but it was very cool. I was very comfortable in my poverty and my vow of celibacy. But being with Dorothy disturbed that, so we talked and she helped me re-think what I was about.

I decided that it wasn't that complicated and I had no real depth to the vow. So I started to get into much more of a relationship with Dorothy, and she is a wild and crazy lady underneath her calm exterior. I was kind of surprised and pleased, and it was very nice to have the amenities of a little condominium unit. I gradually joined her household, moved in and gave away my motor home. I rented a bedroom in her house and allowed her to stay there with me because she only has one bedroom. So I was giving her a little rent to help make things work out, and I was letting her sleep in the same bed.

There were still some unresolved things in my relationship with my first wife. So I initially had concerns, but Dorothy, who had also been married and divorced, helped me to see that all the steps are new steps and steps forward. So I am continuing to make steps forward. I have a much improved relationship with my children and with my first wife, who is their mother and who I see often when I'm involved with the kids. So Dorothy has been very, very good to me, and living here has been very, very good to me. I have a rhythm now to my life that is very satisfying.

—Brent Stuart

Who Is This Guy?

In January 2006 I kept noticing this man walking up the Songaia driveway, usually two days per week. He would go to the Crows' house. Sometimes he would eat dinner in the Common House and spend the night at the Crows. One of the reasons I noticed him was because he always wore overalls. At that point, I didn't like overalls. They reminded me too much of my childhood in rural Kansas. Overalls were for farmers. Men in the city didn't wear overalls. As this man kept reappearing with Stan at dinner, I finally asked Stan "who is this guy?" I learned he was doing volunteer work for Rites of Passage.

I said fine and didn't pay much attention to him for a few weeks.

Then a couple of things happened. One day I helped the gentleman, named Brent, with a mailing for Rites of Passage. This took place over a period of a few days. During this time, I started to notice Brent's kindness, gentleness, generosity and desire to serve others. We discovered we liked the same types of books, mainly mysteries and historical novels. I remember talking about Horatio Hornblower's books. I had enjoyed reading some of his books years ago. Brent also had enjoyed his books. Besides liking some of the same books and writers, we liked similar movies. Brent had a long list of movies he wanted to watch. He would pick an actor or performer he liked. He would try to find all of this person's movies and watch them. His main interest was female actors. We also both came from a small farming community in the Midwest. Brent grew up on a farm in Iowa and I grew up in a farming community in Kansas. We both had lived in Wichita, KS and then moved with Boeing to Seattle. During part of his stay in Wichita, Brent had lived just a few blocks from my home.

The second happening was my third and hopefully last surgery on one of my feet. This put me in a cast for two months. I was not allowed to put any weight on that foot. I used a wheel chair. The community chose to help me in many ways. I am forever grateful for the kindness and generosity given to me during this period. One of the major things done for me was to build what I call my "runway." My wheelchair could not go down the steps on my porch. So Fred designed and built a paved walkway off the end of my porch that connected to the walkway. Brent and a few others helped Fred with the project. Even with the new "runway" I still needed help to go to the Common House for dinner. On the nights Brent was at Songaia, he would come to my house and push my wheelchair to and back from the Common House.

About the same time, Brent was asked to be a summer intern to help in the Songaia gardens. He moved his small RV to Songaia. He was now at Songaia most of the time. He had been using a 7-inch TV to watch movies. When it broke, it seemed quite natural for him to watch movies at my house. The more we saw each other, the more we liked each other. Around the end of June we started talking about a relationship. At first he was quite reluctant. He did not know what he wanted to do with his life, including whether he wanted to attempt to establish a relationship with his ex-wife. Brent didn't think it would be fair to me to start a relationship under those conditions.

So we remained just friends, but not for long. One night in July 2007, he spent the night with me and he has never left. Although two days later he left on a three-week Journey's trip. So he really didn't move in until August 2007. He pretends he rents my bed and lets me sleep with him because I have no other bedroom. I think one of the reasons he chose to live with me is he loves my adjustable TempurPedic bed. If it isn't working, he threatens to find another woman with a TempurPedic bed.

We didn't tell the community, we were both living in my house. Some members noticed immediately and others didn't even know after several weeks. They would see Brent leaving my home in the morning to work in the garden. They assumed he had dropped by for breakfast. All were happy to have Brent as a permanent part of the community. Since he had already been in the community for a few months, he didn't have many problems integrating into Songaia in another role.

I took a leap of faith in starting a relationship with Brent. I was taking into my home a recovered addict who had little money and didn't have the faintest idea what he was doing with his life. There was a sense I could trust Brent. He is a very kind, caring person, with a generous soul. He is also a very hard worker for the community. He has introduced Nigerian goats to the community and helps care for the chickens. His passion in life is to serve others.

He has brought love and joy to my life. I am learning from Brent *how to slow down and not take life so seriously. He enjoys living at Songaia. We are friends, companions and lovers.*

What about the overalls? He still wears them. I have come to like them. At heart Brent is still a farmer.

—Dorothy Fulton

Courtship in Community

I met Nartano, and I told him where I lived, and he said "Oh, I've always wanted to go there," because he'd been to Songaia before it became a cohousing community. And so I said to him, I have three little children, do you still want to know me? And he did.

The first time he came to visit me at Songaia, we were having a workday, and since he wanted to join in, he was invited to join Doug shoveling horse manure. I remember Michelle coming by, "Well, if he shovels shit, I think he's going to get along with us."

So I think this is the only relationship here that has begun in this context and stayed. I mean Tom and Michelle found Songaia together, I think, even though they celebrated their wedding with the Songaia community. They came as a couple. So I think that's just kind of an amazing thing considering everything that's happened in the marriages that have fallen apart here. Yeah, I came here with George, and he couldn't adapt to this place. He really could not. And I think that faith thing that I had come with, the idea that this was going to work out, and it spectacularly did not for quite a while. And then, now look at it. I have discovered that I can have a community of support despite my life being messed up or what people may have thought I've done wrong. Because at one point I thought I would probably be asked to leave, that everybody is ready to get rid of me, I was causing so much trouble and pain. I wasn't sure that this whole group relationship was going to work.

When we had our wedding here, everybody from the community was there. And everybody helped with potluck and setting things up. This was really incredible! We had a wedding party, and during our wedding party, they came in here and made our bedroom into an exotic love nest. And then, Nartano was required to load me into a padded garden cart and drive me back to our house. That was very funny. Through all of this, I realized that I can be loved and accepted, imperfections and all.

—Sadhana Fricke

Marrying into the Community

I can't imagine how our marriage would work if it had not happened at Songaia. What we are doing, I believe, truly works only in community. We are a blended family. We have a difficult relationship with the father of the children. And our family, being immersed in this flood of love and support, is tremendously benefited by neighbors who check in, especially neighbors who check in when I walk through the commons carrying the weight of the world on my shoulders. "Looks like you need a cup of tea." I'm tremendously grateful for that. We're approaching year number seven, and when I came here, I had virtually no idea what would happen. I went on faith alone.

I came here after having lived most of my life essentially single, definitely without kids, and connected to community in a much different way from how it is now. That was a whole bunch of short stories, casual relationships, and if you didn't get along anymore, well, it's a big meadow with lots of flowers. That's totally different from the kind of life I have here, because Songaia is a whole bouquet of real long stories, stories that we weave with each other. I can't imagine how this would be without Songaia. It's like not even a thought.

It is realizing that each person is living their own individual story and yet, we join, that is where the value of community really comes in. So much of my emotional interaction happens with a whole circle of people here. There are people I am closer to, and there are others I am not that close to. And still, we cross paths, and there is this interaction, sometimes even non-verbal, simply knowing the other person's there.

—Nartano Scharnhorst

Working with Difficult Relationships

Our story would be incomplete if we did not indicate that the diversity of personalities is also one of our greatest challenges. The diversity may present itself in unhelpful ways. Some relationships in community are difficult, just as they are in some families. When one or more individuals become a challenge to other community members, there is often a tendency to avoid encounters with the individual or deciding to care for them with the intent of "fixing" the situation or relationship. Neither of these approaches is generally helpful. Avoiding the relationship perpetuates an unhelpful stagnant situation, while expecting to "fix" the situation is probably an illusion that will only result in further frustration.

If the difficult relationship is isolated between one individual or couple with another individual or couple, it is appropriate for one or the other to suggest a conversation to reconcile any differences. If neither is willing to take the initiative and the tension is affecting the harmony of the community, then a third party intervention or mediation becomes appropriate. If the focus of the difference is related to any existing community structure, such as the landscape or food, it is often appropriate for the committee concerned to take the initiative to work through the issue(s) with the concerned parties.

The intervention or mediation is sometimes conducted by a single person but we have found that a team approach is usually more appropriate. There may be an advantage of a second set of ears as well as a second voice to buffer or reinforce the mediator's role. The intents in these interventions are to create a setting in which listening occurs, needs are identified, and unhelpful or incorrect assumptions are revealed and hopefully corrected.

Collective interventions occur when two or more members, either informally or as part of a committee, such as the Navigators, discern that an inquiry or mediation is required. One of the important aspects of collective interventions is choosing the most appropriate person(s) to be involved. This requires knowing the relationship that exists among the members and choosing the person based on that knowledge. It also assumes that everyone is kept in some relationship and does not become totally disconnected from the community. These interventions are not always immediately successful, but are generally a necessary step towards eventual reconciliation.

Communication Strategies

The health of any community is related to the level of trust among its members. Songaia has worked at building trust among its members through its culture of interaction and by encouraging and facilitating open communication. This presumes or implies that there is a process that is used to enable effective communication to take place. Actually, there are a variety of defined and undefined processes being used.

About three years after we moved in, the Navigators set up two opportunities for members to learn about the Nonviolent Communication (NVC) process. These were well attended and a few members participated in ongoing practice sessions. Barb went on to become a certified practitioner. Although the process was not adopted as a standard practice, it did raise consciousness among members to be more intentional and proactive in our communication with each other.

In our group sessions, a few of us use Technology of Participation conversation and workshop methods. Others draw on various methods they have been exposed to in other group settings, including other intentional communities. During the year we were focused on improving our communication style, we invited Rob Sandelin from Sharingwood, our nearby sister community, to share some communication styles that were working for other communities.

Our communication process is a work in progress. There are those who are passionate about this and work very hard at empowering all of us to be more intentional in our communication. They will often initiate dialogue when that seems needed. There are others who avoid efforts to structure dialogue and will sometimes react negatively to a process like NVC being used in a dialogue involving them. There are some who will engage in dialogue but are reluctant to initiate it. It has been a combination of individual and collective efforts of many adults who took the initiative to intervene when dialogue was considered necessary to resolve or avoid conflict.

Finding My Voice

During the first few years of living in community, I struggled with three concerns: 1) parents were not supportive of having their kids do chores or anything for the community if the kids decided they did not want to do it, 2) I was bothered by the kids making noise at meals in the Common House, and 3) if you were late for a meal there may not be any food left for you. The second banana is supposed to make up a meal for you if you are going to be late, but it does not always happen. After five years, I decided I was not going to put up with these last two issues, so I dropped out of the food program.

The community held a Sharing Circle as people were anxious about the future of the program. I experienced pressure to stay in the program, but I did not agree. You might say I am a shaker and mover. I like to get people to grow. My world is all about living out loud. I fought these three things for years. I then opened up to others that I trusted. I talked to them and found others who had similar feelings. I began to see I was not alone. I then gave myself permission to live out loud. So when something gets to me I will take it to that person and talk it out. For a while people were not validating other people for their thoughts, but as we grew together and trust and love each other for who we are and for being ourselves, we began to validate each other for the gifts we bring to the community.

I also saw early on who was who and what they would do and not do around the community. So I felt I knew what community was about and how some did not want to be accountable or take responsibility. But we are working on this, it will come up again and again until it's the right time to work on it. I love being in the community because I trust these people with my life. I love their support. I realize I need structure and most of the people in this community do not need structure. When I need structure I put it out there. Yes, I do live life out loud. To this day, I still ruffle feathers at times and that is okay. It's like, here I am again, time to get out of your comfort zone. This does not happen very often. I view this community as a big family or a marriage, you have to continue working at it to make it work.

—Kathleen Stern

There are some who may not have particularly good communication skills but are still able to establish healthy relationships with other members. Qualities that contribute to building good relations, other than communication skills, are authenticity, willingness to help, being sensitive and present to others.

The Internet as a Communication Tool

There were expectations after we moved in that the internet would become an effective tool for scheduling meetings and sending out notices. The experiences with email and attempts to create schedules have been mixed, some would say quite discouraging. The mixed results can be attributed to the diversity factor: some members are very comfortable using the internet as a means of various forms of interchange, others are not.

Everyone in the community has the capacity to send and receive email. However, everyone does not want to be expected to utilize email as a primary mode of communicating. One member dislikes receiving community emails because he is immersed in emails at his workplace. Some just do not access their emails on a regular basis. Others are okay with simple emails but do not want to deal with more complex forms of communication, like scheduling meetings and events. These constraints on use of the internet for community communications have been significant. It has meant we could not assume that everyone was receiving emails. Consequently email has had to be supplemented with direct communication for those who cannot be counted on to access their email.

There is also the concern that email hampers communication because there is no body language, tone of voice, etc., and because of this, miscommunication is likely. There is general agreement that emotional discussions should not take place over email. If someone sends out an email that has the potential of stirring emotions they are encouraged to take the discussion off-line.

Honoring Aging in Community

Aging in the larger society is associated with a variety of fears and unhelpful stereotypes. Some fears include failing health, insufficient finances, loneliness, being a burden and a lack of purpose. These fears and the aversion to aging are reinforced by societal stereotypes of seniors as incompetent, physically and cognitively inept and socially estranged. The estrangement is related largely to social patterns that tend to isolate older folks once they leave the workplace, as well as natural patterns of congregating by age. The increased mobility of society over the past 50 to 60 years has further isolated older generations from their children, so the separation is even experienced in families. All of this has contributed to the emerging trend of moving seniors into retirement villages, assisted living facilities, and eventually nursing homes.

These aging stereotypes almost crept into our recruiting images in the pre-development phase but never affected actual recruiting practice. There was a fear that if we had a large contingent of seniors, the physical work of the community would be on the shoulders of the younger members. This has not been the case. Often, the reverse was true, that some younger family members were not as available for construction projects or ongoing tasks, such as food shopping, most of which are handled by senior members. Many younger family members have the demands of children and careers to accommodate. It is true that, as seniors age, they will become less able to take on much of this work, but in many of their retirement years they have assumed a great share of the burden.

Seniors are included and engaged in all community activities to the extent they are willing and able. There have been a variety of helpful interchanges between children and seniors. Mutual respect is the cultural norm.

Old Folks Are Nice To Have Around

I think a mixture of age ranges and age groups is one of the biggest assets of living in a cohousing community. And I think it's really necessary for cohousing. Having people at different places in their lives really brings perspective and it also keeps the community rolling.

I don't think we would have the food program we have if we didn't have our older ladies and retired folks. And I don't think we'd have the same sense of identity and ritual without those folks. It's just like in families. It's often the older ladies who keep the families going. Grandma keeps the family together. And when Grandma's gone, there's something missing. And I think that's what our older ladies bring.

They bring a sense of perspective about our lives. I see my life now with my small child, but I know that there's something else that will happen later, and knowing that is really good. And when there were family problems in the beginning, resulting in divorce, the younger folks were much more judgmental—I was one of those. The older folk's stance was, "Well, that's not a good thing, but people make mistakes." There was more perspective that I think younger people tend not to have. A lot of us, I think, especially people in their 20s and 30s, can be very judgmental. I think the older folks held a helpful balance.

Older community members have also acted as mentors for me. They are people I look to, people who can really listen and who've been where I am now. This is also true for my children. Alaina, my 16 year-old daughter, was invited to go on the Women's Retreat this year, and that was neat for her. Michelle taught her how to knit at the retreat. It was very sweet. Having older folks with us is very, very good. I really appreciate them.

—Danielle Olson

Elders at Songaia

When I was a child, I was, for the most part, freaked out by the elderly. My grandparents lived in other states and I only saw them a few times a year. The elderly were people I saw in stores or on the street, but not as a part of my daily life. How wonderful it is that this is not the case for my own children. In addition to their biological grandparents, my kids have grown up with a wonderful group of "adopted grandparents" at Songaia. The elders of Songaia have nurtured the children, teaching them, playing with them, and working with them.

As in many indigenous cultures, the elders at Songaia are honored for their life experience, their wisdom, and their willingness to share their time and energy with the community. Sadly, I must confess that during the recruiting phase, I was one of those who feared that too many elders would burden the younger members of the community with the bulk of the work. I was, of course, proven completely in the wrong. Not only do the elders have more time to do much of the work of the community, in many ways, they do it better than I with my limited life experience, would have, had I even had the time to do it.

However, community work is only the tip of the iceberg. My children and I have benefited in innumerable ways from what we have learned from our older community members. Elders in our community have helped me to see others' points of views and to be more compassionate in how I treat people. They have offered valuable advice when I have faced difficult decisions or crises. Songaia has changed the way that I see the roles of older people in our society. I am grateful that my children are growing up with this model. Rather than being alienated from the elderly, as I was, they view them as valued, respected and loved members of our community.

—Rachel Lynette

Honoring Senior Transitions

Ceremonies that mark the transitions of seniors are important for some of the same reasons they are important to adolescents. They provide opportunities to declare new intentions as well as to be honored for past accomplishments. Perhaps the greatest value is to give seniors permission to celebrate aging and the new opportunities and roles that are open to them, whether that be as elders, crones, grandfather or grandmother.

I have been honored as a senior in three community ceremonies: the first was marking the beginning of this phase of life with a grand 60th birthday celebration, the second was my initiation as an elder of the community, and the third was my initiation as a "Revered Grandfather," marking my transition from being a physically active elder to a wisdom elder. There will be a final celebration at the time of my death that I will help design. Each was a collaborative event. They are not representative of a community tradition, although in doing them it is hoped that other seniors will allow the community to do the same for them, and in doing so, begin to establish celebrations as cultural patterns.

Initiation as an Elder

I had just finished dinner in the community dining room when the Songaia men folk came bursting in, hooting and howling, dancing around the room dressed in various face masks, with some beating on drums. I was escorted out the door and directed to sit in a large, deep fiberglass wheelbarrow-like apparatus. A couple of the men pushed me as far up into our woodland as they could manage, at which point they helped me out of the vehicle and walked me to a fire circle, where I was invited to sit.

This setting was to be Songaia's first initiation of an elder and I was the honored recipient. I had just turned 70 a week before and shared with the community my declaration of choosing the path of Earth Elder for this latter phase of my life. I announced that I would be doing a three-day retreat from the yurt at Songaia with the intent of connecting to nature and the sacred space that our community occupies. The event took place the day after my retreat ended.

The ceremony began with one of the men calling in the four directions. He described the energies of each direction by relating them to the qualities I manifest in my life and work in the community. Then each of the 11 men present sequentially affirmed my presence in their lives and the role I played in the community. They also expressed their commitment to support me in my new Elder role. It was a very heart-filled experience.

I was then invited to share my vision of this new role, after which it was announced that the vehicle I was transported in was a gift to me along with registration to a one-day seminar on mentoring led by Michael Meade. The event concluded with wild drumming followed by hugs all around.

—Fred Lanphear

Aging in Place Successfully

There is a movement within cohousing networks called "Aging in Place Successfully." It offers the vision for seniors living out their lives in their own residence/community. It explores and considers the extent to which community members can organize and provide the ongoing support that is currently provided by costly retirement centers, assisted living and nursing homes. It is a way to recover, at least in part, the role that extended families have played in previous generations.

Songaia conducted a ten-session study on Aging in Place Successfully in the Spring of 2008. There was a general commitment among the 15 participants in the study to create the culture and structures that will enable seniors to be sustained and empowered in place in their elder years. At the beginning of this series, I presented the community with a real life situation that would test how this could be implemented. I had just received a diagnosis of amyotrophic lateral sclerosis (ALS), often referred to as "Lou Gehrig's disease," a progressive, fatal neuro-degenerative disease in which muscle movement is lost, leading to total paralysis. The average lifespan after diagnosis is 2 to 5 years. I specifically asked the community to be on this journey with me and to support my wife and me to live out my final years in residence. The community committed to this support and some of the specifics of this care are spelled out in Chapter 5, Confronting Our Challenges.

CHAPTER FIVE

Confronting
Our Challenges

Every community, like every family or other social entity, periodically encounters major challenges along with the struggles and irritations that are just a part of everyday life. Some of these are predictable, such as members experiencing major health issues or ultimately death. Another predictable challenge is the impact of family separations and divorce on community life. The impact of members selling their units and new folks moving in is another. Some challenges may be totally unexpected, such as a lawsuit, but must be dealt with when they occur and should be prepared for as ultimate possibilities. Struggles and irritations can become major challenges if they get out of balance, i.e., they accumulate or expand and require major correction.

This chapter describes my experience of how our community encountered these challenges, how we responded, and what we learned and would recommend from our experiences.

Family Separations and Divorce

It is not surprising that family separations and divorce have been a part of our community life, as it reflects a national trend. About one in every three of the founding Songaia families has gone through a divorce in the nine years since moving in. It is possible that the additional stress of living in community may have contributed to these divorces, or perhaps the lack of a common commitment to be in community was a factor. It has also been suggested that living in community makes it easier to divorce because of the extra support that is available for a single parent. Whatever the cause, the impact of the separation and divorce on the community was stressful.

Each divorce was unique and impacted the community differently. In the first separation and divorce, the husband moved out but the wife stayed with her three children and remarried a few years later. In the second separation that also led to divorce, the husband moved out and within a year the wife and two boys moved into a development about a mile away. In the third divorce, the couple attempted initially to live on different floors of their Songaia unit, but this didn't work. The mother and daughter then moved close by and continued to be a part of the community. Eventually the mother connected with a partner and moved out of the area, but close enough for the daughter to visit with her dad on alternate weekends. In the final family divorce, the spouses initially took turns staying at Songaia so that their kids had a steady homelife in the community. They eventually moved out when one of them was looking to buy a new home with a new partner. In two of these situations the spouses have remained connected.

Each of these divorces was a wrenching experience for community members who found themselves connected to one or both spouses as if they were family members. It was not apparent to many of us that any of these families were having marital troubles that would lead to divorce, so there were no intervention efforts and likely would not have occurred in any case, unless the marriage difficulties were disrupting other community members. Nor were there organized community responses to these divorces, only individual expressions of support were offered. During the development stage there was a ritual to acknowledge the divorce of a member family that they requested. This ritual was very helpful in establishing the continuing relationship of each to the community, as well as publicly acknowledging their new relationship. In retrospect, it seems that it could be helpful to do a similar ritual with each divorced family, but there has to be a willingness by the divorced couple that often does not exist.

Divorce can and will likely be an intrusion in the life of community, just as with sickness and death. The challenge may be twofold: how to provide upfront support and perspective in shaky marriages and how to reduce the trauma to families that end up in divorce.

Upfront support is often found through male and female bonding that can occur in community, either in men's and women's circles or in one-on-one relationships. This support may take the form of encouraging marriage counseling or by providing adult companionship, helping to buffer a difficult marriage relationship.

Sale of Residential Units

We feel fortunate that we have only had two units sold between 2000 and 2010. When someone does put their house up for sale, the experience is like someone from your family moving out of your household. One of the first questions is: why are they leaving? Were they not happy living here? The other big question is: who will buy the unit and how will they fit into our community?

Both units that have been sold were owned by families that had been through a divorce. The first unit went up for sale in the third year after we moved in. A real estate agent, a friend of the former member, was hired to sell the house. We were anxious that whoever bought the house should know what to expect and what would be expected of them. The agents, who happened to be a husband-wife team, were invited to meet with us so they would be knowledgeable about the community and how to present cohousing to potential buyers. We emphasized the importance of finding buyers who want to live in community. Fortunately, a family came along who had been looking for a community so we had a good fit.

Assimilating a new family into the community does not happen naturally or necessarily easily. There are community patterns in place that the residents take for granted, while newcomers will first need to recognize those patterns and then decide how to participate. We had not prepared a process for welcoming and assimilating a new family at the time they moved in. Rachel, who knew the family, offered to be the community contact person or host. Craig and Karly, who shared their duplex, were asked to meet with them to review our written and unwritten processes and protocols. Tad, Cyndi and their son, Lucas, were welcomed to the community at one of our dinners, but there was never a formal welcoming ceremony like we do for new associates. The orientation and assimilation process took place gradually over the following months.

The second resale was by another of the four families that went through a divorce. The title of the unit was held by the former husband who was remarrying and planning to purchase a new residence. This required selling the Songaia property. Songaia Association exercised the right of first refusal clause it has in its agreements with all members. The Association had two weeks to locate a buyer. There were six families lined up as potential buyers. Craig offered to act as the arbitrator and was able to work out an amiable agreement for our newest member, Jean Mohr, to purchase the unit.

Jean had been a member of New Earth Song Community, Songaia's sister community, located on a half-acre adjacent parcel, that was in the forming stage when she bought the house.

She was not a stranger and, from the community's perspective, was assimilated as a member of the community quite rapidly.

When Irritations Get Out of Balance

There are times in the life of a community that irritations accumulate or expand to a point that they become a challenge that must be addressed. Some of these are perennial problems that show up periodically. Others are more specific and rooted in a particular situation.

One of the perennial or reoccurring irritations at Songaia is the perception, as well as the reality, that community work is not being shared by all of its members equitably. This is a challenge that is endemic in (cohousing) communities. We have approached this challenge both structurally and culturally.

One structural approach that has helped is organizing workdays and directly approaching members, inviting them to participate or asking them to commit to doing the work at some other time if they can't make it to the workday. Another solution was to allocate the ongoing work activity of appliance repair, which was consuming much of our in-house "fix-it" member's time, as a function of Common House care, thus relieving the member who handles these repairs from the normal Common House cleaning assignment that other members receive. A third approach was to propose hiring outside services to do the work. This is acceptable when the work is more technical than our members want to handle, but there is resistance to accepting this as a community pattern, particularly by the members who already do more than their share of work.

This brings us to changing the community culture in regards to work. We do have different values and patterns around community work. In general, most members favor doing the work that we are capable of doing rather than hiring it out. That usually works because we have had enough members who build community work into their weekly time line. However, there is a tendency for those who do work to contribute to expect that others will do their share. One way our community story is told reminds us that work distribution will never be equitable in community. Another part of that story says that those who don't participate are missing out on the joy and satisfaction of contributing to making their home a great place to live.

Over time the temperaments of some members become the cause of intense irritation that may require mediation. This may occur among members who are working on the same project but can't agree on how it should be done. When this happens a third party may offer to intervene. Other times, one of the members, knowing there will be difficulty, will proactively organize informal meetings to sort out issues they are facing. One, or sometimes two, of our trained Nonviolent Communications (NVC) facilitators and others will be asked to help mediate a difficult discussion with another member. This self-organizing approach to resolve anticipated conflict has been a creative alternative to repeated confrontations and given us the tools to use at a later date.

There have been a variety of strategies members have used to cope with irritation or antagonism. Avoidance is frequently a default mode; however, we encourage ourselves to use face-to-face dialogue as the first response. Another creative approach is to anticipate and structure responses that alleviate potential irritations. This requires an awareness of individual propensities and the willingness to self-consciously prepare intentional responses. This willingness has been encouraged as the community's trust level has increased and individuals have taken on a greater sense of responsibility for making the community work.

Responding to a Lawsuit

It came as a great surprise to the community and to each of its members to be served with papers that charged us with breach of contract with a former member who left the community following his divorce. Not only was it a surprise that we were being sued, but also what we were being sued for not doing. Songaia was being sued for not allowing the former member to construct a greenhouse behind his unit. It was our understanding that we had authorized him to go ahead with this project, but that he failed to follow through on the project.

A community task force led by Brian was assigned to take the necessary action to respond to this legal charge. A defense lawyer was hired and in working with him we proceeded to pull together all of the documents related to interactions around the "breached" agreement. It was a time consuming task but quite satisfying that we were finally able to access all of the documents that were needed. It was one of those occasions that we were very thankful for all those who had taken notes and filed them in such a way that they could be retrieved.

We were also thankful that we had Officers and Directors Liability Insurance that covered all of the legal costs associated with this case. This insurance covered each of the community members as well, because our legal structure names each owner-member as a director of the board.

When the case was heard in County Courthouse, many of us attended to provide support for those who were testifying and also out of curiosity and a desire to be present at this unique event. It had all of the formality and suspense of a TV court drama. The difference was that it was happening to us and it was very real. As the hearing unfolded, we first listened to the case against us presented by the attorney and our former member along with supporting testimony. It was difficult not jumping up to object, but we all patiently waited our turn to testify. When we started to present our side of the story, it was difficult not to clap and cheer for our attorney and each Songaia member who was called to testify. At the end of the day we were told that the judge would deliberate on the merits of the case and present his decision at a later date.

When the judge presented his decision that supported our claim that there had not been a breach of contract, we were obviously delighted. We wanted to celebrate, but it was clear that we had mixed emotions about what we were actually celebrating. It was certainly not a sense of victory; in fact, there was sadness around the losses the former member must have experienced. We finally did celebrate the collective work and the particular roles that community members played in achieving the verdict that established that we had operated in good faith to our agreements.

Community Lawsuit

The letter came just before the anniversary of our third year living together at Songaia. At first, I thought it must be a joke, but when I had read through the legal documents for the third time, I realized that we were in for a long road. In the end, the lawsuit would be dismissed, but getting there took over three years and often frustrated, confused, angered, challenged and exhausted us. It also drew us closer together. Now it seems so clear that part of growing into community is walking through difficulties together, supporting each other along the way. At the time, though, it felt like just a long, hard road.

A key turning point for me came during the most challenging stretch of the journey, right before the trial. The community had gathered to hold a support circle for the "legal task force," the small group working with the lawyers to prepare for the trial. During the circle, community members spoke to each of us in turn, affirming the gifts we had brought to the process so far and committing themselves to support us in the work ahead. I recall feeling such a powerful sense of acceptance and love from the group, regardless of what might happen at the trial. The road hadn't gotten any shorter, but it seemed like we had walked to the top of a rise together, the road stretching out before and behind us. In that moment, my eyes lifted beyond the asphalt at my feet to see the whole landscape, clear and precious and beautiful. I carried that moment with me for a long time, like a light in the dark.

I recently found an email from early in the lawsuit that seems rather prescient now. It said, "That's the overview [of the legal situation], at the moment we have met our responsibilities to begin the process and we now just need to hang on (and hold onto each other) for the ride." We did, and in doing so became community in a richer way.

—Brian Bansenauer

Health Issues

There have been many opportunities for the community to come together to create a care structure for someone going in for surgery, having a baby, or other special needs. In each case, a "care circle" was held in which most members of the community were present. The "care circles" each have a facilitator who orchestrates the discussion. It begins with the person who will be receiving the care describing the nature of the health issue and the specifics, if known, such as date of surgery and rehabilitation therapy required. The facilitator then asks in what way the community can provide support. These requests can be very specific or more general in nature.

Specific requests have included providing transportation for medical care, building a wheelchair ramp to the front door, and installing a washer-dryer in the unit that was expecting a third child. The material costs for these projects were covered by the recipient, but the labor for constructing the ramp and installing the washer-dryer was contributed by community members. A more general request was for persons to be available when needed to assist in physical therapy exercises following knee surgery, or to walk with a member who was instructed to walk for exercise.

When a member is going for surgery there will usually be a healing circle in which community members gather and share in a healing ritual. These healing circles do not occur as the result of a committee mandate; instead, they are the outcome of a culture of care. Generally, someone steps forward and organizes the circle in conjunction with another member.

Long-term Care

The community participated in the 10-week course "Aging in Place Successfully," which explores the notion of community being a place to live through the end of life. Around the time the course began, I was diagnosed with ALS, a degenerative and terminal disease with a 2-5 year life expectancy. This provided an opportunity for the community to apply what they were learning, as ALS care can be provided at home, but does require an intensive care structure as the disease progresses.

As recommended in the course on aging, a "Share the Care" team was formed to coordinate care from the community, family members and friends. The community often talked about this as an opportunity, not an obligation. Individual members stepped forward to take on the responsibility of coordinating the "Share the Care" team, and each week people in the community signed up for different care roles to help distribute the workload so that it did not become a burden to just a few.

Individuals also offered their personal skills in response to many lifestyle modifications that needed to take place. Most of the community found a way to participate in the care, whether it was constructing handicap aids, serving a meal, or helping get me in or out of bed. Three community women worked with me on a weekly basis to provide bodywork to keep my joints limber. Cindy did yoga therapy, Jean did a full body massage, and Michelle an active body exercise each week. Helen, a Songaia

Associate, joined in the weekly process, contributing stretching therapy. Other folks came occasionally for massage and exercises and to assist in other ways. Visits by community members to provide physical care were often used as an opportunity to check in with me about my spiritual state of being.

The experience of providing long-term care brought about huge changes in our community of Songaia. It has encouraged new relationships and connections with each other and has brought children into the circle of caring. We discovered that it is possible to age in place successfully. We have all become more present to the priceless experience of daily living, even death and dying.

Embracing a Terminal Illness

In December 2007, I received a diagnosis of ALS, better known as Lou Gehrig's Disease. A month later I requested a community circle to share my diagnosis with everyone and to ask for their support as I moved into the last phase of my life. During the sharing circle I offered an image of my condition as an adventure and invited the community to be a part of it.

Over the course of the next three years, as I progressed through various stages of ALS, I experienced increasing levels of care from members of the community. During the first year, as I struggled with the growing loss of strength in my legs, people in the community helped by creating handicap aids that enabled me to get in and out of bed, use the shower and adapt to a reclining chair, to name a few. Others stepped up to assist when I had fallen or to help me in and out of the car. It was a time of experiencing my vulnerability and learning to receive community help. Toward the end of the first year the community decided to celebrate my life while I was still able to participate. It was a grand celebration where individuals were invited to share their memories and good wishes with me. I felt blessed, honored and cared for so deeply.

It was during the second year that I became confined to a wheelchair and required a mechanical lift to get me in and out of my chair and bed. This involved a lot more assistance to help my wife Nancy operate the lift, adjust my equipment and move me as needed. As I began losing the strength and control of my arms, my dependence on the community continued to increase. Perhaps the most poignant aspect of this dependence was letting go of my personal privacy as I gradually became unable to manage my basic bodily functions by myself. Although there were some community members that expressed their discomfort in assisting at this point, there was no shortage of people that elected to help out as often as necessary.

In the third year, I had lost the use of my arms and could no longer feed myself. I needed to have someone with me at all times now as I was more and more relying on breathing equipment and was not capable of using the phone. I was now totally dependent on 24-hour assisted-living care, with most of this provided by community members, along with a part-time home care aid, my wife Nancy and my family.

Throughout these years, I experienced the community, children as well as adults, as my extended family as they did what they were able to meet my needs. I could not have chosen a more perfect setting for this final adventure.

—Fred Lanphear

When Death Happens

Death can happen unexpectedly. The community was shocked one Sunday morning in November 2009, when Stan, one of the initiating members of Songaia, died suddenly. Some community members were immediately available to assist when the aid ambulance arrived and in taking his wife Carol to the hospital. When resuscitation failed, many other community members gathered in the emergency room around Stan's body and circled with the family in the initial stages of grieving. Following a prayer by the hospital chaplain, we sang "Amazing Grace" and the "Irish Blessing" along with statements affirming the completed life of our dear friend and colleague. A grieving circle took place that afternoon in the Common House. The following Monday evening at dinner, candles were lit around the room and community members continued to remember and celebrate Stan's life. The following Saturday a ceremonial circle was held in the Common House to reflect and share people's experience of his loss.

The response of the community was like losing a family member. People reached out to each other to console and for consolation. In the midst of expressing our gratitude for Stan's life, we recognized and acknowledged our deep gratitude for each other. We experienced a new level of trust and connection.

In January 2010 the community collaborated with Stan's family and other organizations to create a wonderful memorial service. Songaia children and adults gathered in the front of the church and sang a beautiful, unrehearsed rendition of "Song of the Soul." In a testimonial to Stan it was noted that the evening before he died, a sharing circle was held in which he named our community journey as *inventing* ourselves in the first decade, *growing* ourselves in the second decade, and *reinventing* ourselves as a community in the coming decade. It was as if he was passing the torch to the next generation.

CHAPTER SIX

Working Towards a Cooperative Model of Sustainable Living

A lmost as daunting as learning to live together in community is the challenge of how to do that while living lightly on the land, or being ecologically sustainable. As a society we have been programmed by the marketplace to be consumers. We consume as though there were no limits on resources, and throw stuff away as if there was some "away" place that will not have some impact on our planet. We purchase commodities that often come with more packaging bulk than the commodity itself. Some of us have been taught gardening practices that rely on chemicals for pest control. We have been programmed to believe that every adult or teen needs their own car. Our challenge is unlearning and changing our ways of living in relation to the earth as if our very lives depend on it—because, in fact, they do.

The Challenge of Fulfilling Our Value of Living Lightly on the Land

As stated in our Development Program, which was prepared and published between 1993 and 1994:

> "We will endeavor to deeply understand and improve our economic (consumption and production of natural resources) relationship with Songaia, the earth, and our non-

human co-residents of this particular place and planet. Developing this understanding will require study, attention, and vigilance. We expect our relationship to develop over the coming decades—for converting this desire into serious action will only be achieved through a mature, long-term approach toward the creation of a sustainable lifestyle."

As described in Chapter 2, we came together like most co-housing communities, with great ambitions to build a community that would be friendly to the environment. Many of our early dreams of using alternative forms of sewage waste disposal, green building materials, and alternative forms of energy were bracketed because they would have made our project financially unviable. We have not lost sight of our dream and continue to look for ways of living lightly on the land. We recognize that we must re-educate ourselves and come to a common understanding of what needs to change and to make the necessary investments to make the change happen.

How do we re-educate ourselves? We hold sharing circles in which we discuss how we can collectively reduce our vehicle use or discuss other ways we can become more sustainable as a community. In those circles, we look at what we have accomplished, what we are working on, and we see ourselves in 10 years. We operate as a sustainability support group: discussing what we do as individuals and families, encouraging each other and suggesting things to consider. We have held three courses in the community focused on care for the earth: an 8-session discussion course on "Discovering a Sense of Place," a 9-session discussion course on "Deep Ecology," and a 5-session course on "Elders as Earthkeepers."

We participate, individually and collectively, in seminars and other events that provide technical and practical information on becoming more energy efficient. When an idea for a project occurs, various members bring their individual expertise together to evolve the most energy efficient solution. An example of this approach was the decision to install a solar-powered pump in the water fountain at the garden. Accomplishing this objective utilized the skills of four members. In this process we are evolving a collective conciseness around the notion of energy efficiency.

Exploring Sustainable Agricultural Practices

One of our great assets is abundant land and water that supports our desire as a community to grow fresh, organic produce that can be served in our common meals. Gardening is not everyone's passion, and we learned in the formative years of our community life that it does not work to require everyone to contribute a stipulated time working in the garden. Fortunately, some of our members chose Songaia because of their desire for gardening and the tremendous opportunities this community offered them to fulfill their passion.

The Biogaian Committee is the group of passionate gardeners that take responsibility for the gardens and landscape. There are usually 5 – 6 members who voluntarily serve on the planning committee and a few others who will join in and take on particular gardening tasks when needed. We have a large garden, many berry and fruit tree plantings, and extensive grounds to maintain. We have also introduced chickens and goats into our agricultural practices. Our dream is to learn how to become more self-sufficient in case that should ever be required. Until then, we work at producing as much of our own produce as possible and enjoy the fruits of our labor and the satisfaction of working on the land and enjoying the connection.

Crop Production

The size of the vegetable garden, 120' x 110' (0.3 acres), is intimidating to many of our members. Recently, we have been focusing our attention on how to make the garden more user-friendly and inviting to those who are not passionate gardeners. We have divided it into four quadrants, with one designated for family plots, one fallow for most of the year, and the other two for community crops. Each quadrant has been divided in half with a walking pathway of wood chips. A moat was dug around each quadrant, lined with black plastic and filled with wood chips. This defines the quadrants while reducing weed and slug encroachment into the crops.

The family plot quadrant and one of the community plot quadrants are divided into 3' wide beds with 1.5' wood chip pathways. The beds are watered with soaker hoses that are attached to a manifold at the ends of the beds that can be controlled individually. The other community quadrant is used for growing squash, cucumber and pumpkins. Because of the wide spacing between these plants, they are individually watered with drip irrigation and mulched in between plants with large cardboard sections from furniture stores. The cardboard is left on the ground over the winter and peas are sown in that quadrant the following spring. After the peas are harvested, that quadrant remains fallow for the rest of the summer and the chickens are brought in to eat the pea vines and other weeds that come up during the summer.

Availability of fruit is a high value at Songaia. The first year after construction was complete, the Biogaians selected, purchased and planted a variety of small fruits and fruit trees. The small fruit included strawberries, raspberries and blueberries. They were planted along walkways or near the Common House, where they were conveniently located to encourage grazing. The fruit trees were located on the south and west borders of the main garden. They include peaches, European and Asian pear, apples, plums and apricot. A few espaliered fruit trees were planted on the trellis in the public plaza, and grapes were trained to grow along the top of the trellis so they were more accessible for grazing. They are cared for by the Biogaians with a passion and skill for managing these crops.

The selection and management of particular vegetable crops is again based on the passion principle. In winter we meet and discuss which crops individual Biogaians are willing to take primary and/or secondary responsibility. We may discuss the value of growing some crops based on community needs, but if an individual is not willing to step forward to manage the crop, it will not be included in our crop selection.

Once crops are selected, the crop manager decides which varieties and how many seeds of each to order. This is communicated to the person ordering for the committee and the community in general. Starting transplants from seed may be handled by one person for everyone. This is done in our propagating house located on the west side of the barn. We use artificial lights to start those seedlings that are planted in late winter or early spring. Once the weather is suitable for moving them to the garden, the crop manager takes over the transplanting, watering and care of their particular crops.

Integrating New Practices

Another sustainable practice includes raising chickens, integrating them into the crop production. We developed a chicken tractor, basically a chicken coop on wheels with some movable fencing, that could be used in the fallow part of the garden for weeding and fertilization. Families take turns harvesting the eggs from the coop, a week at a time. There are not enough eggs produced to supply the community's needs, so families take turns having fresh, organic eggs to eat. The chickens were initially raised from chicks until they started laying. They are kept for about 18 months after they start to lay and are then slaughtered and replaced with 12 new layers.

As new people join the community they often bring with them new ideas and skills and the passion to implement them. Brent, who grew up on a farm in Iowa, proposed raising goats to help control the proliferation of blackberry bushes. The community agreed and has benefited not only in blackberry eradication, but has also become enamored with the goats, particularly in the birthing, care and raising of the kids. A year later, Brent suggested that the community raise bees, resulting in the community's first beehive. Along with the bees came the bee lore, the bee movies, the history of apiaries and many walks to visit the new hive. Another family, one of the new Associates, raised the possibility of growing shiitake mushrooms in the woods on the property. Each of these new ideas has added interest, viability and renewed energy to the community's efforts at sustainability.

Service and Sustainability

Imagine the impact. Visualize how it feels to harvest the food that will feed the community for dinner. This was my family's introduction to "Service the Songaian Way," and as new associates, our fulfillment from this experience inspired an idea that would help us give back in its own way.

My wife, Katie, and I pitched the idea of leading a project to grow shiitake mushrooms in Songaia's forest. The project would be long-term, and would benefit the community over a period of several years if successful. We planned to inoculate 14 logs that would come from a Maple tree designated for removal due to health and city mandated requirement. We discovered that these logs could grow mushrooms for up to 5 years, and that production could yield as much as 100 pounds of mushrooms a year. The project expense: $70 in materials. The experience of the community participating in the experiment: invaluable.

The project was approved by consensus, deemed a great learning opportunity and potential addition to the diversity of food grown. Equally, it created an opportunity for Katie and me to add value through service in a different way, and symbolized our appreciation for Songaia. Looking back, it was easy for me to get lost in the possibility of how many mushrooms we could yield and feed at Songaia. Yet when our work par-

ty began, I was quickly reminded of why the project was so important. The experience of working together with the intent of doing something for the benefit of everyone was what the community cared most about. Mushroom production was of far less importance.

We appreciated this experience and lesson in service and sustainability as a symbol of Songaia. Its very identity is uniquely formed by each person within the community, and how they choose to contribute. We chose mushrooms...and we look forward to expressing ourselves and experiencing the community with this different perspective.

—Michael Stein

Challenges

One of the challenges we have experienced from year to year is who will harvest the crops once they are ready. The crop managers generally are not interested in harvesting. The cooks do not want to take on this additional task. So we have experimented with designating someone to discern when crops are ready to harvest and then notifying the community until someone comes forward to take specific responsibility for the particular harvest.

There are other challenges along the way, such as coordinating watering times, getting someone to care for a given crop when the crop manager is away, and getting help when the task is more than the crop manager can handle by him or herself. One of the incentives for others to participate in the gardening is the fact that the upfront costs for the garden come out of the food program. Any produce grown in the garden contributes to reducing the cost of the food program, which consequently benefits most of us.

The Role of the Garden Manager

The vision of a sustainable garden integral to the community food system included a knowledgeable person with sufficient time and energy to manage the gardens as their primary role. For years the community had operated with individuals taking on the garden duties in part-time, fractional ways, but we lacked continuity throughout the year. This vision became possible when Patricia, a Master Gardner and an original member of the founding community who had moved away and then moved back to the Northwest, became excited about the possibility of taking on this role as part of a year-long experiment. It quickly became clear having a full-time manager facilitated continuity of production and harvest and gave people a way of seeing how the garden could become a significant part of our ongoing sustainability. This in turn has elicited greater interest and involvement in the garden.

Developing a Sustainable Food Program

The Songaia food program has been one of our most successful sustainable strategies. It contributes to sustainability through reduced packaging, reduced transportation from producer to table, overall reduced costs and increased use of locally grown produce. The strategies include bulk purchasing, selective shopping, utilizing Songaia produce, and effective team-work by the Fabulous Food Folks (FFF). There is no paid staff even though there are weekly duties and monthly duties that have to be done in order for the program to work. The weekly workload is distributed among members of the FFF. This includes one member identifying menu requirements for the week and informing two other members who manage the food inventory and do the weekly purchases. Other members of the committee contribute to the planning and guidance of the food program as the team strives to fulfill the values of healthy eating and sustainability.

In addition to the five community meals provided each week, families can obtain most of their foodstuffs for their other meals from the community pantry. This includes dairy products or non-dairy alternatives, yogurt, butter or margarine, eggs, cereals, fruit, bread, most dry goods and some canned goods. Families have to buy their own meat, vegetables, desserts, soda pop, beer or wine for their in-home dining. A family could exist on items from the community pantry alone if they chose.

There have been shifts in the values that drive the program since its beginning. Local purchasing has become a higher priority in recent years. Organic produce has been a primary consideration from the beginning but never a mandate. Because of the need to juggle many values, including cost, the criteria for buying organic was to prioritize and reduce the purchase of produce known to have the highest pesticide residue.

There are three stages of purchasing: bulk buying, weekly shopping to meet menu needs for the week, and occasional single item purchasing when something is missing. The bulk purchasing is done once a month by phone to a wholesale distributor who delivers by trailer truck. The weekly shopping is done by FFF team members who purchase milk, yogurt and cereal based on orders from each family, as well as items needed for the community meals. The shopping is done at 3–4 locations to take advantage of greater selection of organic produce and better pricing through quantity purchasing. Although this is time consuming, the cost savings and the elimination of multiple family grocery trips make it worthwhile.

Other Sustainable Practices Along the Way

Community Exchange

In addition to the bulk food purchasing program, we have a community exchange of household consumables, like toilet paper, liquid soap and other cleansers, that works in a similar way. These are purchased each month from an eco-friendly wholesale distributor that provides our foodstuffs. These products are stocked for families to buy as needed and billed each month. The cost savings from bulk purchasing is transferred directly to the unit.

Community Laundry

A choice we made in the planning stage was to discourage each unit from purchasing washers and dryers by providing a common laundry facility. In fact, the design of the units did not include space for them; however, we did allow a couple of exceptions for families with numerous children. What we did provide were two commercial stacked washer-dryer units in the basement of the Common House to supplement an existing single washer and dryer unit. A sign-up sheet for the use of laundry has been a simple but effective way to accommodate family needs.

Recycling

The practice of recycling seems basic to sustainability, yet it is far from simple, particularly in a community setting. From the time we moved into our units we have had general agreement to practice recycling. The infrastructure in our county is very supportive of recycling and the community has taken advantage of this, but the criteria and method of processing recycled materials changes periodically. This frequently leads to confusion and the need for re-education, particularly of the children who often take stuff out to the rubbish and recycling dumpsters.

The recycling of vegetable waste products has been an objective from the time we moved in. We have four worm bins at the Common House that have been used to handle the waste from the kitchen. Other practices include feeding the vegetable waste products to the chickens and hot composting, a labor-intensive method that speeds up the composting process.

Composting

In addition to the worm bins, we compost weeds and other vegetable waste from the gardens in a couple compost piles.

These are turned yearly when we rent a tractor with a front-end loader. Every two to three years the composted soil is moved to the plant nursery where it is stored until needed for potting soil or other use. Woody materials from pruning are removed to the woodland, as they take much longer than herbaceous materials to decompose.

Reusing

The reusing of clothes, toys, and household goods is another sustainable practice we encourage. A give-away table located in the cafe allows for books, puzzles and other household goods to be exchanged among families. Larger items are often placed in the barn or on a front porch with a give-away sign. This sometimes contributes to the need for an annual barn purge. Items are also reused when community members request an item. This is particularly appropriate for items needed for special use or limited time, such as camping equipment.

Community Patterns that Reduce Vehicle Use

The community is the hub of activity, and subsequently members generally travel less frequently. There are activities that engage people so they do not have to travel as much for entertainment and other social activities. When there are events outside the community, members will often carpool.

Wood Shop

The wood shop is located in the barn and consists of power tools from some of the families in the community. They are made available for common use by the adult members of the community. Hand tools and various hardware items are kept here as well. The availability of the tools and work space enable the community to build and repair many community projects, such as the benches for the Peace Garden, the trellises in the plaza, and the playground structures.

The biggest challenge in the wood shop is to ensure that tools are returned to the shop when they are removed for a project. Similarly, putting tools back in their proper location has also been a challenge. Failure to do either of these has been the cause of consternation and threats of refusal to make private tools available for community use. It is a pattern that is difficult to change because it also happens with one's own private tools.

Emergency Preparedness

Another approach to sustainability is being prepared for emergencies. An emergency preparedness group was formed in early 2009 to create reliable backup systems, get reserve supplies in place, and develop a complete written emergency plan. It is recognized that after these goals are achieved, it will be necessary to have an ongoing training/preparedness program, rotate supplies, update documentation, and generally maintain our readiness.

Songaia emergency systems are being planned at both individual unit and community levels. The most common emergencies include medical crises, accidents, winter storms, fallen trees, power outages, flooding and fire. Rare but possible emergencies that could affect Songaia, including earthquake, epidemic, natural gas leak, septic failure, toxic contamination, geologic/volcanic disturbance, high-voltage mishaps, and all acts of violence will also be assessed with possible responses considered for each.

We recognize that all of the outside support systems that help maintain life here are important; most are essential, and therefore require back-up systems and reserve supplies in case the systems we depend on should fail. Our goal is the seamless integration of the following systems with community life: water; food; medical, fire safety and emergency services; sanitation; power and heating. Special needs of families are also being considered.

New and Future Projects

Harnessing the energy from the sun continues to be a vision that beckons the passion of our facilities team. The first small scale, low investment opportunity was to provide solar energy to power a very low wattage light to extend the day length for the chickens so they would continue producing eggs during the winter. A solar panel mounted on the chicken tractor accomplished the task and was our entry into the world of solar power. The second opportunity, also on a small scale, involved providing solar energy to power a submersible pump in a water fountain located in the center of our garden.

A much larger solar energy project is being considered that would provide passive solar energy to heat the water for the laundry in the Common House. The proposal suggests that if each family would put its tax rebate towards the cost of purchasing and installing the solar panels it would make a major contribution towards energy efficiency as well as stimulating the economy.

Another project strategy that is being investigated is to organize an LLC that would acquire and operate a fleet of energy-efficient cars and trucks for its members. This strategy should allow the community to reduce the number of vehicles that are owned collectively and have the most appropriate vehicles available to meet the variety of short and long distance travel requirements most efficiently.

The opportunities for moving towards a more sustainable way of living are numerous. The increased energy efficiency is multiplied by the collective nature of the community. We are only limited by our ability to imagine what is possible and to mobilize the resources to make the opportunities become real.

CHAPTER SEVEN

Creating Sacred Space in Community

What Is Sacred Space?

Sacred spaces are those special, magical places where one experiences a profound connection with "wonder" or mystery. Sacred space may take the form of a beautiful garden that takes your breath away. It may be in the woods, in a grove of trees or in a babbling brook. Or it may be in the community commons where Maypole dances are held each year and snow people are created each winter. The reality is that sacred space is in the eyes and experience of the beholder.

What defines sacred space may have many roots. It may be the connection with a person's deeper meaning in his or her life, perhaps through symbolic association with a person or experience from the past. It may be in the designation of the space as a memorial to a deceased loved one. It may be in the experience of creating it or in a joyous or meaningful occasion that has taken place in the space. In some way, it is encountering the "holy place," where you experience a reality other than that which occurs in your ordinary daily life. It is space that heals the spirit and which integrates and makes whole our connection with the earth and life itself. Ultimately, it is discovering and/or realizing our connection to the universe, our "kinship with all things," that enables us to participate in celebrating creation itself.

There are those spaces that are perceived as sacred by many, while others may only be experienced as sacred by a single person. If it is the latter and the intent is to make it sacred to others as well, then conveying the story of what makes it meaningful may allow others to have a common experience. Experiencing sacred space in community can take place physically, as in celebrations or community work projects, or spiritually, by sharing personal stories about a place in the community that has taken on a special meaning. This chapter will describe those special places at Songaia that are perceived as sacred by many or just a few. The community-wide experience is discovering that "sense of place" on the land that creates an enduring connection.

Developing the Landscape

Land Use Planning

We were blessed with 10.7 acres of land, including 4.5 acres of a beautiful, second-growth Douglas fir woodland on a western-facing hillside. This woodland provides a gorgeous backdrop to Songaia as you enter from the main road. The edge of the woods opens onto a gently sloping meadow with remnants of an earlier orchard and woody ornamental nursery sprinkled across the landscape. An irrigation system was in place for the nursery when the property was purchased and this determined the location of our current vegetable garden, west of the Common House. The three major use areas and their location are the woodland on the upper eastern third of the property, the residential cluster and common facilities in the central third, and meadow, garden and orchard on the lower western third.

There are other use areas such as the education area that supports the Rites of Passage programs and Fort Can-be, a wetland, and the sustainable agriculture area.

Preserving and Featuring the Natural Resources

A high value has been placed on recognizing, appreciating, and preserving the beauty of the existing natural features on the land. Before construction started, two of the Biogaians walked the land and marked existing vegetation that we hoped to preserve, some of which was in the proposed residential area. When the plants selected for preserving were shown to the construction project manager, we were disappointed that he only promised to preserve one cluster of trees in the residential area. However, it was symbolically significant that the preserved cluster was an aspen grove which is interconnected through its root system, making it a kind of "tree community," and it is a "singing" tree, as the leaves make a fluttering sound when the wind blows.

The Songaia woodland is the focus of one of our greatest efforts in preserving our natural resources. It is not virgin woodland. There are two septic drain-fields in the woods, one near the center and the other on the edge. Fortunately, existing trees were maintained in place and only the underbrush was removed and continues to be removed. By mowing the drain-field at the edge of the woods we created a park-like setting with huge, glorious evergreen trees. Unfortunately, these trees are more vulnerable to windstorms, as the tree roots have been disturbed by the trenching used to install the septic drains. We lost seven huge trees during a great wind storm in 2007.

The woods are not used on a daily basis, but ongoing maintenance is required. One of the Biogaians has committed to taking care of the woods as one of his projects. This involves clearing and renovating pathways as well as planting additional native trees and shrubs. Values that inform the development of the woodland as well as the managed landscape are biodiversity, beauty and providing an outdoor laboratory for learning about plants.

Development of Residential Unit Landscapes

An integral part of the community landscape is the limited common space around each residential unit. The landscaping of these areas is the responsibility of the owners of each unit. There have been a variety of approaches in creating the unit landscapes. One member who particularly enjoys gardening offered to select and install plantings for the front or back yards of her three most immediate neighbors. The neighbors, who were not so keen on yard work, were happy to pay for the plants, and everyone got to enjoy the landscape. Another approach was to hire a member who was a landscape designer to design and install the landscape plantings at a relatively low cost. About one-third of the owners chose this route. A third approach was for individual homeowners to design and establish their own landscapes and this was done by about one-third of the owners.

There are relatively few constraints in the landscaping of limited common space. Any trees to be planted require checking with a Biogaian to make sure the selected tree is appropriate for the site. There are also restrictions on erecting visual barriers between neighbors. These are the only specified restrictions. Some yards have covered and open patios, others are without grass. All have a variety of flowers, shrubs and fruit trees. Each yard reflects the unique values and tastes of its owners, resulting in a rich tapestry of diverse expressions.

An Evolving Organic Process

Songaia's landscape has continued to change since construction was finished and the units were occupied. Unlike institutions and many planned communities that create and complete a finished landscape at the time of construction, Songaia has evolved its landscape as a visible sign of its unfolding dream. The landscape that has developed is quite different from the conceptual designs created during the program development. In those earlier plans the public plaza was planned as a more formal garden and gathering space than how it has developed. Instead, the community vegetable garden has become the more formal setting. These shifts reflect the value of living on the land and allowing the form to organically develop.

Community patterns and perceptions have both informed the development of the landscape. Watching where people congregate and keeping track of circulation patterns has been very helpful in deciding where to locate plantings, benches and lighting. Learning about member perceptions in sharing circles has also been important. The diversity of perceptions range from a desire for more openness with few trees to wanting a canopy effect with tree-lined walkways. It has been a creative challenge to find a balance. We have encouraged members to fulfill their particular needs in the way they design and manage their limited common space.

Community Gardens

Vegetable Garden Evolves into a Potager

The vegetable garden has been a continuing project from the time the community was a residential learning center to its current form. It was a strong attraction for a few members, so helped recruit folks for the Biogaians. Sustaining that passion in the form of expenditure of physical energy has been challenging. The scope of responsibility is huge.

The garden has gone through a number of changes, partly related to shifting priorities of the Biogaians, but also due to the shifting context and reaction of the community to the gardens and landscape as it impacts their life. At a sharing circle in 2005 focused on the garden, it became clear that members were intimidated by the expansiveness of the garden. With that awareness, the Biogaians moved towards creating a more intimate garden.

The first stage was to divide the gardens into quadrants and within each, to create beds 3' x 26' with wood chip paths separating the beds. This helped greatly and enticed a few families to sign up for family plots. The next challenge was how to tempt them into the garden. A possible solution to this came in a sequence of three events.

The first event was meeting a plant collector who was looking for space to plant her rose collection. The second was obtaining a large 3-tiered Italian fountain when five Songaia families purchased an adjacent residential property. The third was the introduction to the concept of the Potager, an ornamental-vegetable garden, in a book that mysteriously appeared in the Common House.

The Potager design consists of rock-sand pathways dividing the quadrants that run north-south and east-west with the water fountain at the intersection in the middle of the garden. The fountain is under a gazebo with benches that surround it and support climbing roses. At the entry points are trellises with symbols for the direction they represent. The roses are planted along the pathways and on the borders of the quadrants.

Peace Garden

In 1995, during our self-development stage, we were selected as a site for a Peace Pole by the International Peace Pole Project. The pole was erected in front of our current Common House. The pole has the following phrases printed on the poles: "May peace prevail on Earth" and "May peace be in our homes and communities." This site had originally been designed as a Japanese Garden with a 40+ year-old Dwarf Cut-leaf Red Japanese Maple located in the center. This location was just waiting to be transformed into a Peace Garden.

The process of designing and implementing this garden is described in Chapter Three. It has continued to unfold organically during the subsequent years, with the addition of dwarf ever-green shrubs, herbaceous perennials, and spring bulb plants. Each spring the garden's special caretaker weeds and adds shredded bark mulch that makes it appear freshly cared for. A bubbling fountain was added in 2006 along with two wooden benches adjacent to the fountain. This has become a node where two to four folks can sit to converse. It is also a good place to meet and talk about Songaia with guests who are interested in community.

Public Plaza and Playground

The Peace Garden is within the public plaza that extends out from the Common House. The plaza is bordered on the north by a trellis with a raised planter box to provide soil to support espaliered fruit trees, grape vines, and herbaceous annuals and perennials. The planter box was necessary because the plaza is located over what was once a graveled parking area. The planter box also serves as a sitting bench.

The big attraction in the plaza is the playground. It is used daily by the kids, after school, before and after dinner, and frequently during the weekends. Occasionally an adult may be observed on the swings. The three swings are, at times, all in use. The sacred quality of this space appears to come from both its functionality and its visual statement. The play structure is a visually appeal-ing art-form and the free-form flowing pattern of the curbing makes an equally strong visual effect. The texture and contrast-ing color of the wood chips is also pleasing. The initial concern of some that this would become a cluttered eyesore has been alleviated. To the contrary, it is a form of community art.

Other Sacred Spaces

The Labyrinth

Located behind Units 1 and 13, the labyrinth had a bumpy jour-ney before it became a functional reality. Initially, the idea of a labyrinth was to be in association with the vegetable garden. The plan was to mow a section of the meadow on the south edge of the garden, layout a labyrinth, and use small fruit shrubs as the divider. The area was mowed and staked out. When the beds to be used as dividers were tilled, it became quite clear that it was going to be challenging to establish the small fruit shrubs, and even more challenging to maintain these plantings. The project was abandoned.

A few years later the notion came up again, with the stipulation that it be low maintenance. Red bricks set in the ground were chosen to divide the pathways. Although they did not originally submit the proposal, Chuck and Marilyn stepped forward and took responsibility to make it happen. Initially they obtained about 800 bricks that were available for whoever would come and pick them up. Chuck engineered the design and coordinated the actual layout of the Cretan style labyrinth. Both have maintained the labyrinth by mowing regularly and using a weed whip over the bricks occasionally to uncover them when grass conceals them.

The labyrinth is only used on occasion, but visitors will often ask if they can walk it. Visiting children sometimes decide to walk or run around the labyrinth. When we gather for some rituals, the labyrinth often becomes the choice location because of its circular nature and the positive energy associated with it.

Woods and Nature Trails

The trails have been in place in the woodland from the days of the earlier RLC. They have to be cleared about once a year and recently steps were added in the steepest sections. People are drawn to the secluded nature of the woods and the anticipation of coming across some unusual wildflowers or four to six-legged creatures. At the appropriate time of the year, trilliums can be a delightful surprise that makes the walk through the woods a very special event.

There is an enchantment the woods provide that makes it a unique and magical place to visit. As surrounding wooded areas are being lost to development, the Songaia woods take on the feel of a last refuge that needs to be preserved at all costs.

Fort Can-be

In the springtime, a tiny stream of water empties into a series of contained pools. Following the stream uphill reveals that this stream was dug by trowels to divert spring water from the hill to places below. The children may jump into one of the little ponds and take a mud bath. This is one of many activities that can be seen at Fort Can-be.

After a windstorm that dislodged huge evergreen branches, a lean-to appeared. On one occasion all the children were actively engaged in digging what was proposed as a future garden. The nearby pile of woodchips became a place to dig deep to release the steam from the composting and a place to play "king of the hill." This sacred place is defined by the many creative activities that go on throughout the year.

The establishment of Fort Can-be never went through the decision board process nor was it included in the master landscape plan. It just showed up as a demonstration of childhood enthusiasm and invention. It is not used nearly as much as the playground in the plaza, but it is no less special to the children.

Songaia's Fort Can-be

"Follow me this way to the historic site of Fort Can-be."

Lucas led the way. Soon, we were across from the Common House and under the low branches of towering evergreen trees.

"We worked a year and a half on this fort," said Lucy.

Similar to excavators of ancient antiquities that disappear with the passage of time, the group paused over the partial remains of the once sturdy fort, made from a discarded giant cable spool, branches, sticks and mud. The fort had announced to all: "This is our territory, our place!" When has building a fort not thrilled a child? These children were no exception. Their voices rang with energy and pride.

"We have actually had several different forts here," pointed out Christopher. "One was not big enough and we tore it down and built another one. We even built one that looked like a beaver's den without water."

All the children talked at once about their adventures building the forts, getting bored, tearing the forts down and rebuilding something even better, and about how the forts led to an even greater challenge.

"Remember the time," began Lucas, "when we decided our fort needed a source of water? You see, we needed a river, a stream—well, water close by. So look what we did." He pointed to a large dug out mud hole and then to a four to six-inch wide trench of similar depth. The trench continued up the hill through the green ferns, huge trees and thick underbrush of the forest and then out of sight.

"Up here is where the springs are," injected Amelia. Off the group scurried, over and under the dark green ferns and bushes, following the curving trench beside, around and among the giant trees.

Suddenly, all stopped. "The ground's always damp here," Christopher showed me. "It's an underground spring. Over here, the water hits the surface." And sure enough it did.

Lucy added, "We really worked hard on this trench—all of us. During the summer, we met after lunch and worked until dark everyday until it was finished."

"Yeah," chimed in Ian, "and Christopher, he announced at dinner in the Common House—"

"The Fort Can-be stream is unplugged today!" Amelia shouted victoriously. "Yeah, water flows!"

—from Childrens' Interview

The Yurt

The 24' diameter canvas yurt located in the outdoor education land use section is the primary structure for the Journey's
programs, but it is frequently used for solstice ceremonies by
the community and for other activities with a focus on nature.
It was also used as the base camp for a vision quest when I prepared myself to become an Earth Elder.

The yurt is on a raised wooden platform and has a Plexiglas
dome that can be opened when the heat builds up during the
day. At night the stars and often the moon are visible, providing
a sense of camping under the stars. Although the yurt is only
used on special occasions, the very nature of those occasions
has elevated this location as one of the sacred spaces, at least for
those of us who have used it.

The Sweat Lodge

At the edge of the woods just east of the public plaza is a dome-
like structure about 5' high and 20' in diameter. It is constructed
of Red Alder saplings covered with black plastic. When being
used, this sweat lodge is also covered by many blankets that con-
tain the heat generated by the red-hot volcanic rocks that are
introduced into the enclosed structure to create a sauna-like
ambiance for healing or prayer circles.

The volcanic rock becomes red-hot in the fire pit just outside
the entrance to the lodge. The ceremony of the sweat lodge has
established this as one of the sacred places at Songaia. The lodge
was built by Stan and volunteers from the Journey's program
that conducts rites of passage. It is an extension of the Journey's
program space and the use of the sweat lodge is coordinated by
Journeys. Many of the "sweats" are open to community members. Over the years many Songaians have participated in one or
more sweat lodges.

In conjunction with the lodge and fire pit is a small, 3-tiered amphitheater that is sometimes used for outdoor rituals or ceremonies by Songaia. Mostly, it is used for Journey's programs.

The Tree House

The tree house up in the woods was built by Craig and his 20-year old son, Zeph, about a year after the move-in. This was the fulfillment of a long-standing ambition of Craig. It was built between three trees that form a triangle at the 20' level at which the platform was built. The platform was built out of treated wood and has a rope fence that contains anyone standing on the platform. To reach the platform, one has to scale a vertical ladder-like structure made of triangular hand-grips that also serve as steps. Beneath the platform a heavy-duty rope is suspended and can be used for swinging out into the open wooded area.

The children are attracted to the tree house because it represents adventure and even a bit of danger. The children know better than to go there alone. Although attracted to the tree house the kids don't seem to have a sense of ownership of it. They have talked about building "their own," but the adults have convinced them that they can modify the existing one and make it more their own.

Discovering a Sense of Place at Songaia

Each of us has some special connection to the earth. For some, that connection is with a land or water feature from our childhood. The memories of such places never leave us; the memory of the smells, sounds and physical features are still vivid to us in our older years. It is as if that place was like an umbilical cord that nurtured us with the natural order of things.

We do not outgrow our need for a sense of place. We often become disconnected from nature as we spend most of our waking hours in offices, cars and houses. Some people never even get out of their cars to walk to the house, but electronically open the garage door, drive in and enter the house from inside the garage. Being in nature has a healing quality that can only be understood through personal experience.

It is that connection and/or re-connection to nature that we strive for in our design and care of the Songaia property. It is quite evident that the children have a strong sense of place at Songaia. Our "free range" children explore and connect to the multitude of natural features at Songaia throughout the year. When there is snow, the children are up and out in the snow early in the morning, making snow people or forts even while the snow is falling. When the springs on the hillside start to flow, they are there with their trowels to create diversion trenches. A fallen bird and even a dying plant is a "call" for intervention.

The adults are also connected to the natural landscape and experience that sense of place that "roots" them to the property. For some, it may be the landscape and gardens around their unit; for others, it may be the family plot in the community garden, or the labyrinth, the Peace Garden, or the woods and commons that connect us all. Whatever feature each of us identifies with, the common thread that helps tie us together is a love for the land and a commitment to protect and preserve it.

The Detention Pond

Lucas was in charge. "Over this way to the historic detention pond!"

The group picked up momentum. A few ran, others skipped or hopped. One little girl declared excitedly to the younger visitor about her same size, "These are the grasses where the fairies live."

"There are no such things as fairies—no real fairies," the little boy stated firmly.

"How do you know? This is only your first time here," she threw over her shoulder as she scooted over the edge and down the 10 foot drop to the meadow. He scrambled to follow.

At the edge of the drop off, I abruptly stopped. Chris, considerably ahead of me, shouted while pointing his finger, "Jump down right there!"

Wait a minute! Can I really do that without seriously maiming myself? Ian quickly sensed my hesitation. "We have some stairs," he offered.

"Oh yeah, come this way," Lucy volunteered. While not missing a beat, she guided us around a cottage and down the stairs into the winter-dried grasses of the meadow. The grasses were high. Certainly high enough for fairies, the thought flittered through my brain.

We headed toward a large cyclone-fenced area and through a gate. The detention pond was a bowl shaped area that the County built years ago for water catchment in times of heavy rainfalls. The children couldn't remember a time when water stood in the bottom. Three goats baaed from a rocky rise. Then, they trotted eagerly toward us to greet the children and to receive hugs and pats. Ian introduced me to Bella, Cookie and Delight, and proudly showed me a tiny protruding horn on the head of one goat. I was impressed, impressed by the easy rapport shared by both the children and goats, by the warm sunshine and by the calm that settled over all of us.

"So, here it is, the detention pond—where the girls crawled through the pipes from here to the brier-patch up there in the meadow," announced Lucas.

"Up where?" I turned and looked back up the hill. "Humph, that was quite a crawl."

"Yup, and all underground, too!"

"Who did it and what was it like?"

Lucy stepped forward slightly. "Three of us crawled the pipes: Risa, Natasha and me. We were about eleven. It took us several days to plan what we wanted to do. I think Natasha went into the pipes first."

"I didn't crawl through," admitted Alaina. "I stayed here in case they needed help. If there was a problem, I was to go get someone."

"We were fine. It was gross, though, "Lucy said, with her face scrunched up tightly. "It was disgusting, dark, wet and there were lots of

slugs, crunchy, slimy slugs. Since we did the army crawl, slug slime was all over our fronts. And, we heard lots of weird underground noises, too."

"Whenever anybody talked down into the tunnel to us, it was really echo-y and cool," Natasha added. "A couple of adults saw us climb out and before we knew it, the adults put bars and rocks over the pipes, so we couldn't do that again. Good times, really good times!"

—from Childrens' Interview

CHAPTER EIGHT

Realizing Our
Larger Purpose

Community Outreach, one of Songaia's seven values, has guided our community since its formative stage. Our decision to use the cohousing model, rather than more traditional forms of intentional community, was partially related to the cofounders' intent of impacting a wider section of society in a style that more people could relate to as a possible way of life.

Telling Our Story

The community has recognized and accepted its role as an alternative lifestyle that would be scrutinized and featured in the public and academic media. In the '90s, before we actually became a cohousing community, we were featured on a local TV show as a contemporary form of the historical "Utopian" communities. Since we have become established as a cohousing community we have been featured periodically in local newspapers. The timing is either associated with a local activity, like when we moved into our new homes, or when a national article on intentional communities catalyzes the local media to look for similar activity in its geography. These have generally been positive experiences, particularly for the children who love to see their photos in the newspaper.

On a few occasions we have been scrutinized from an academic perspective. In 2001, we received an inquiry from Adam Wilson, a Dartmouth College student, about the possibility of being a case study for his thesis. He wanted to connect with us by engaging in community work, meals and other activities prior to interviewing us individually. There were a few members who were reluctant at first because they didn't know anything about this student. It wasn't long before Adam won his way into the hearts of everyone. After spending the summer with us, inspiring us with the amount of work he accomplished, he returned to Dartmouth and wrote his thesis, which most of us read, experiencing our lives and chosen lifestyles being affirmed. All of us at Songaia fondly remember Adam and frequently talk about finding another Adam to join us.

On another occasion, we were honored with a week-long visit by author Graham Meltzer, who was investigating and comparing the sustainability of the design and practices of different cohousing communities on the Pacific Rim. He interviewed us as a group, giving us the opportunity to learn, often for the first time, other members' perspectives and experiences of living in community. Although there was some anxiety about how the community would be described in his book, there was a sense of pride and excitement when the book was published and Songaia was portrayed positively.

On a less formal side, each of us continues to tell our story about Songaia and cohousing. When people ask where we live, it's an opportunity to tell our story, for those of us who like to tell it.

Food Shoppers as Cohousing Ambassadors

Friday morning, first stop is Cash and Carry, a local warehouse store – we walk into the store and are welcomed over the intercom – "here comes Marilyn and Nancy – all hands on board – they are now on aisle 5!, check them out." Or at Trader Joe's – "wow, you certainly buy a lot of milk! You must feed lots of folks!" We often respond with, "We live in a cohousing community with 38 folks and eat 5 meals together each week." Chuck is always ready to tell our story if the clerks even hint at a curiosity question about our shopping practices.

—Nancy Lanphear

Tours and group visits provide a great opportunity to "show and tell" what community living is and what it isn't. We have hosted a number of bus tours since we moved in and often do individual and small group tours. We frequently serve lunch to bus tours to give folks the opportunity to experience and learn about our food program. After lunch, we tour the garden to see yet another dimension of the food program. The garden includes both community and family plots as well as a chicken "tractor" designed to fertilize and cultivate each of the garden plots. The tour takes people through the multipurpose building which houses private storage units, arts and crafts studio, food pantry, indoor recreation space, woodshop, garden equipment and bicycle storage space.

What Do Your Friends Like About Coming to Songaia?

This time it was Nancy who posed the question: "What do your friends like about coming to Songaia?"

Natasha answered first. "My last visitor to Songaia was Dylan. And it was amazing! It was an unusual night. We all sang together before dinner while Kevin played his guitar. During dinner, we listened to a reading of one of Fred's favorite authors. And, Dylan was like "Wow! This is like heaven!" Songaia folks were very friendly to him and seemed to really, really like him. It wasn't until later that I was talking to one of Dylan's friends, who said, "Yeah, I hear you live at a really cool place." "Yeah, I do!" I said. His mom and some others have asked me about Songaia since, and I've tried to explain. They say things like "Oh wow, I don't know my neighbors at all." And, "It's cool; you have like a big, big family—lots of people you can rely upon!"

"When I stayed the night over at my friend's house, her family thought we were a little weird, you know, because everyone's all friendly and we do lots of singing," said Lucy. "One friend said she feels really protected here, very safe."

"Um, uh, guys don't really talk," admitted Chris.

"All they do is play soccer and then that's it," agreed Suzanne.

Alaina quickly added, "Well, I heard Christopher's friend getting excited about all the space that is here."

"Yeah, space for playing soccer," Chris nodded.

"I like," said Lily, "going to my friends' houses 'cuz they have cable TV. We don't have it here."

"Well, there is so much more to do here than watch TV!" declared Amelia. "There is always someone to hang out with—even animals to touch and cuddle. We create our own games like Bench, Slip and Slide and Ping. And, remember the car wash we held to raise money for fireworks for the 4th of July? We're always doing something fun!"

"Yeah, and don't forget our forest—we have a forest!"

—from Childrens' Interview

Involvement with Groups and Associations

Our outreach does not revolve around a common mission. Instead, the community supports its members as they engage in individual or group ventures. One of these, the Journeys Rite of Passage program, has been hosted and supported by Songaia from the very beginning in 1987. It was the primary vocational focus of Stan Crow, one of Songaia's founding members.

Over the past 20 years, hundreds of children and their parents have been impacted by the program and by the connection to the community. The community has allocated a section of the property to serve as a base camp for the programs. The children and their parents arrive at Songaia for orientation before the children embark on 1- to 3-week wilderness treks, sometimes spending the night camping in tents on the property. At the end of the treks, the children return to Songaia for a re-connection ceremony with their families. Most of the older children in our community have been involved in at least one of these programs, so there are obvious benefits to the community beyond fulfilling our outreach value.

In the early stages of the program Journeys was primarily the focus of one individual member. However, over time the community has taken pride in supporting the programs and adopted it as a part of our outreach.

It is not uncommon for community members to invite organizations they are affiliated with to meet at Songaia for special events. This has included musical groups, spiritual retreats, and planning meetings, which provides numerous opportunities to expose the wider community to Songaia. These groups usually meet in the Common House, where they encounter our kitchen and dining area as well as our community logistics and "Decision Board." These occasions frequently prompt visitors to ask questions of the member host that provide an opportunity to tell the Songaia story.

In conjunction with NICA, the Northwest Intentional Communities Association, Songaia has made its Common House available as a venue for a variety of public events, such as workshops and presentations generally focused on community life. Some events have attracted 30-40 or more participants, often including community members. Each of the events attracts a different audience that broadens our exposure.

Neighborhood Outreach

When we submitted our rezoning proposal to the county in 1993 we were located in a Suburban Agriculture Zone. Three months later, the Growth Management Act took effect and we found ourselves zoned as an Urban Growth Area. This has impacted our neighborhood in the past couple of years, with massive development of over 500 new homes and new challenges as well as opportunities. Some of our members have worked with neighbors, organizing public meetings, often at Songaia, with developers and county officials, to consider how to reduce the negative impacts of growth and add amenities, such as sidewalks, improved traffic controls and a local park.

A Role in Neighborhood Development

After living here for a few years, I decided to do something about my wife's concerns.

She said, "Songaia's really nice, but it's like being on an island in a sea of concrete. We've got all this traffic, no sidewalks and no parks. There are new developments all over the place, but our neighborhoods are not getting any beneficial infrastructure. We have all these roads and houses, but you have to drive to the store because nothing is in easy walking distance."

Her comments made me think about an earlier experience I had, in which a community mobilized itself to form an educational cooperative. I believed we could do something like that here.

I thought it could work here because of the environment we were in. This included a common house and hence a place to hold meetings, but it also included supportive neighbors. In addition, there had been some groundwork done by a retired civil engineer, who had conducted an extensive analysis of the neighborhood development plan and identified many of the issues that were not being addressed. I thought we could invite the neighborhood, send out flyers and say "If you're interested in parks, if you're interested in having safe walking, mass transit, or in trying to improve your neighborhood so that it is more livable, please come to this meeting." It worked, and we did a meeting every month for five months and on a less regular basis for the next couple of years.

One of the challenges was deciding on how to organize our meetings. Since this was an effort Songaia members supported, Stan and Fred came and talked to me. They both had a lot of experience facilitating and organizing neighborhoods. However, I didn't know this until they told me. They had a whole methodology called Technology of Participation or ToP. The results of ToP were fantastic. In only one meeting we had a common vision for our neighborhood. In the next, we were able to identify the obstacles, or underlying contradictions, that had to be addressed for our vision to be realized. In the third meeting we created strategies to overcome those obstacles and worked to achieve the vision. I was extremely impressed with how fast we came up with a plan for improving our neighborhood.

In pursuing these strategies a lot of things happened. A key strategy was working with our County Councilman. This included Songaia hosting a fund-raising party for him so that we could keep him in office. Our other strategy was hosting a large annual meeting for the general neighborhood and inviting local politicians and developers.

As a result of carrying out our strategies, we were able to accomplish two to three major objectives. First we were able to get sidewalks approved and installed within a year. Second, we were able to have the County install traffic lights at our busy intersections. Specifically we were able to have two put in place along 228th in the first year, and have a third put in place at 212th the following year. Finally, we obtained $5 million for a park. The site has already been selected and purchased. All of this would have never have happened without the support of Songaia.

—James Olson

Songaia's impact on the wider community is not limited to visitors. Some of us participate in NICA gatherings and other organizational events where we share our community patterns and practices. Our community is known for its love of singing. We encourage other communities and groups to sing at every opportunity. Occasionally we go as a group and sing to others, whether at a nursing home, another community or a public event. We also take every opportunity to share stories about our food program.

Our community celebrations with outside guests often revolve around our members. Dorothy held a retirement party in 2006, inviting colleagues and friends from her workplace, church and, of course, Songaia. It was a grand occasion and many of our members and some of the children pitched in and got the gardens, grounds and Common House ready "for company." The guest experienced our life together around a great meal followed by a concert on the Commons, provided by Dorothy's son's musical group.

Connecting with the Broader Community Network

We have a strong commitment to support both the intentional and cohousing community movement. As a community we have hosted board meetings of both the Fellowship for Intentional Community and the Cohousing Association of the US. The FIC meeting was held in conjunction with The Art of Community Northwest Conference in September 2006 and attracted more folks than usual. Hosting the group was challenging, but generally was experienced as an opportunity to meet and learn from other communitarians.

Embracing Our Story

Our life together is our purpose and our message. Songaia strives to exemplify intentional community as a prototype for sustainability. At the heart of this message is the recognition that there is an interdependence of social and ecological sustainability. Many of the practices require a common intent and cooperative action to succeed. Creating a context that bonds us to move collectively towards attaining this value requires many sharing circles, participation in the inspiring programs that we host, and rehearsing our story as we lead tours or just answer a guest's question.

There is a community benefit from doing outreach. It nurtures and sustains a sense of pride and ownership among those who participate in telling the story of Songaia and leading tours. There is also greater responsibility towards helping the community achieve its higher purpose. A way to see this in action is to hold a public event in which the community is on display. It is a great strategy for engaging the maximum number of community members and an effective way of "polishing" the community.

To measure how we influence the wider culture is a difficult task. We only know that we are recognized as those who have chosen a lifestyle that requires hard work, cooperation and letting go of many mainstream values, but that we also experience many joys in community that are beyond measure. There has evolved in our 10 years together a sense of becoming a more sustainable way of life for the future. What we are doing is not just for ourselves, but also for the larger society.

CHAPTER NINE

What Lies Ahead

The dream of Songaia does not have a closing scene. Nor does it end with everyone living happily ever after. Instead, it continues to unfold in a variety of ways that results in expansion, diversification and proliferation. Some of the changes are unique to the characteristics of Songaia while others could happen in any community. The changes bring both advantages and challenges.

Changing Demographics

One thing is certain: our community changes daily as we age. As we approach the end of our first decade of living together, and the second decade since our early beginnings, the new demographics of our community have shifted. Most of our children have now become adolescents and pre-teens, and many of our adults have become seniors. This reflects a shift in energy, leadership, and how we interact and get things done. There are two major concerns: what happens when there is no longer child energy, and how do we care for seniors in their final years?

There has been a reduction in involvement from some adults due to aging and health and an increase in involvement from some of the children. The decrease in adult involvement was expected, but there was no assurance that the children would assume greater responsibilities. The teenagers have stepped into mealtime responsibilities during the week and some of the 10-12 year-olds help prepare the Saturday morning breakfast. Some of these same kids are fully active committee members.

Growing the Community

Since the early development stage, Songaia has cultivated a culture around the image "Friends of Songaia." These were folks who lived here during the 10 years of development but were not interested or able to become members. It includes individuals and families who were once members who withdrew but wanted to stay connected. It includes folks who thought they might sometime become members or just wanted to be associated with what we were doing. These folks come to celebrations, workdays, and occasionally will join us at meal times.

Our Introduction to Songaia

My wife, Katie, our two children and I became acquainted with Songaia not long after Stan Crow, a beloved member of Songaia, had passed. Our first tour of the community had echoed this feeling of loss. It was clear Stan was not only a community leader, but also a man with vision for the community. Songaia's union was represented by the emotions felt as we toured through. Our experience this day was the beginning of our passage to experiencing the meaning of deep, "sustainable culture" and community.

We were greeted on our first tour by Brian. I remember him smiling and embracing our children as we passed by the chickens and he pulled out some eggs. We walked through the grounds of the property to learn its history, meet the goats, meet community members and realize the meaning of sustainable culture. It was clear the community was close. The mural of Stan was a reflection of this, as were the tears shed by the mention of his name.

We were introduced that day to other community members who shared with us their own view of community and life. Each of them was equally eager to hear our story about why we were interested in Songaia. Discussions over dinner offered a glimpse of community life. They laughed, sang songs and offered announcements. I remember be-

ing shocked to later learn it was normal for most of the community to meet five days a week for meals. Even more impressive was that meal preparation considered dietary restrictions for each member and child in the community. You were thought of whether you are a vegetarian, omnivore or allergic to all things dairy.

As we repeatedly visited to learn more about Songaia, I was struck by how open and heartfelt the community was at their community events and with each other. Several associates (individuals and families who don't own homes in the community) and members often spoke of the challenges faced in community, as well as the rewards. We participated in multiple work days, often volunteering independently each week to help clean up and plant in the community gardens. We also led a work party to start a shiitake mushroom growing farm, attended various community meetings and dinners, including circle meetings and a tree ceremony honoring the trees before being harvested. I could sense reservation from some community members by our involvement, perceiving us as being over-eager for community. But it took multiple visits and a lot of discussion with community members before we really started to grasp the community's fundamental focus, which Katie and I defined as "sustainability."

Some members focused more on sustainable culture, others on environmental sustainability, and others on financial sustainability for the community. The more we engaged, the more hooked we became. It was but a few months before we became associates of Songaia. And we are still students, learning how the community practices consensus building, meeting facilitation, organizing work party days, all while working together collaboratively. We are learning that community can be messy and challenging, and also the most rewarding opportunity for growth and communion. We look to our future at Songaia without expectation... and with the belief that we are here to be in service to each other.

—Michael Stein

Some of these relationships have continued since we moved in. Each family develops their own unique relationship to Songaia. Liam has the longest history of those who became associates. He originally was a member; later became a renter; which is a type of associate; then returned with his partner, Karen, to become associates. They have had family garden plots for the past few years. In addition to caring for their own plot, they pitch in and help with other community garden projects. Even before we moved in, Liam took responsibility for keeping the septic drain field clear of brush and has continued to do that for the past 10 years. When they come to work in their plot, they frequently will join us for dinner. Liam, a healthcare social worker, will often join us for care circles to assist us in knowing what's available within the healthcare system.

For the first seven years, the associate category was relatively informal. With greater intention given to encouraging individuals to become associates, it was decided that greater energy was needed in defining the privileges and responsibilities of associates, as well as formally accepting them as associates. This turned out to be a long and tedious process, taking place over the period of a year.

It's Not Just About a Place to Live

I was looking for a place to live, and I called a friend of mine, who said, "I know this house that you might be interested in. It's part of a community, Songaia, and some of the members formed an LLC and bought this house." I called Craig and when I asked about the house for rent, he said, "It's not really about just a place to live, it's about community," and he guided me to the Songaia website.

When I came to see the place, I talked with Craig for a couple hours that first visit, asking questions about the philosophy of Songaia: "was it a cult?" "was there a religious persuasion?" "what was the expectation around involvement and time requirements?" among many other questions. He showed me the place, telling me about the process of becoming involved and that they really wanted people who wanted to be part of the Songaia community.

He said I needed to come to six community activities and needed a sponsor before I could apply to be a member. At this point I would be interviewed by residents, and then be voted in (or not). Nancy said she'd sponsor me, I just needed to check with her before coming to events and let her know I was coming. I attended some dinners and enjoyed the process of meeting people. When I agreed to take the room, there was a stipulation that because I hadn't completed the whole process, the agreement was that I could rent space with a six-month grace period. If I decided I wasn't going to be part of the community, then I'd need to find another place to live. I moved into Alpaca Place in April 2007.

Before I went through the process of being accepted, I was encouraged to seek out everybody, particularly the people who don't come to things very much, so they would know who I was and a little bit about me. I had to write a letter of intention in response to the question, "What do you bring to the community?"

I was concerned. "What if they don't want me?"

Craig said, "Well, I don't think you have to worry about that. That's why we have the process...by the time you have been here six times and met all the people, it's pretty self-selecting. If you want to be part of the community, then we're happy to have you. If you don't want to be, then you've pretty much decided this isn't a fit and off you go."

So that was good to hear. They all voted me in.

The next step was feeling my way knowing that I wasn't a resident—so where was my place? I was very aware of not wanting to step on people's toes. At the same time I wanted to be helpful. So I asked: "Where can I be helpful? Where can I be actively involved within my comfort zone and be needed?"

This has been a good place for me to make some life transitions. My kids had grown up and moved out of the house and I also decided to quit my job then move to a new location on top of everything else. To

have a network of people, this instant family, has been really reward-
ing. Yes, it's been a really good experience and I am glad to be here
and glad to have the relationships with everyone who is a part of this
community.

—Kate Arden

The need for an associate status became clear with the pros-
pect of actual participating neighbors. When an adjacent property (fondly known as Alpaca Place, referring to the local live-
stock) became available, a group of five Songaia families got
together and purchased it, with the intent of preserving it for
Songaia-friendly, community-related purposes. After some refurbishing, the building was rented out as a shared house, with
the explicit intention of incorporating the renters into Songaia
as essentially full participants.

Incorporating "neighbors" raised questions about what Songaia facilities the Alpaca Place renters could use and under what
conditions? Were some Songaia events open and others closed?
What participation was allowed or expected? Some decisions
seemed easy: Can the renters participate fully in the food program, work in the garden, come to game nights? Others were
not so straightforward: How about participation in meetings,
circles and retreats?

A small task force formed to ponder these conundrums.
Meanwhile, another task force undertook the same questions
for anybody not living next door who might want to participate in some of Songaia's culture. Eventually sets of guidelines
came forth, were duly accepted, and sent out for a trial run.
These agreements were the result of separate efforts, conceived
in different contexts, but never coordinated. As a result, various
inconsistencies and inequities (centering on privileges, responsibilities and costs) came to light shortly after our first prospective
associates began the process of applying for membership.

There was confusion about what privileges the various categories of associates should receive. After multiple drafts of the associate proposal the rights and responsibilities were eventually determined. It was a challenging process but it opened the door for new ways of expanding our community.

In addition to Kate and Susie, the first renters at Alpaca Place, and Liam and Karen, others formalized their associate status. Alex and Marna's family, who live about 10 miles away, join us for dinner once or twice each week. They also participate in other activities and committees. Kevin, a neighbor on the edge of the property, joins us at meals even more frequently and helps with cooking and cleaning occasionally. He also participates in other activities. His young son, Cory, comes often to play with the Songaia children. All the members of New Earth Song, Songaia's newly forming sister community, who were not already residents became associates.

New Community Connections

In 2006-2008, new commercial housing developments were springing up all around us. One development took place two lots north of us, in which 20 large houses were built on less than five acres. We were disturbed by this type of development and wondered if we could influence how the lands not yet developed around us might be developed more creatively. We were particularly concerned about the 4.3 acre lot immediately north of us. Some of our members decided to recruit folks who were interested in forming a new community that would be affiliated with but legally separate from Songaia.

A core of 6-8 people came together and formed themselves as New Earth Song community. This effort was spearheaded by Craig, a Songaia unit-owner, along with Patrick, a renting member of Songaia. The initial property strategy was to purchase the 4.3 acre lot to the north. When negotiations for this property failed, they turned their attention to other available adjacent properties. There was one lot immediately south of us for sale; however, attempts to negotiate a reasonable sale price failed. Another option was developing a small community on the Alpaca Place plot. The negotiation for this property was fairly simple, as the owners agreed to only recover their investment costs.

The formation of the new community involved extensive planning and the creation of their own identity. A major part of this was establishing a collaborative relationship with Songaia and keeping the Songaia membership fully informed of their process. It was understood that any of the members of New Earth Song have the opportunity to become fully participating associates and all of the current members have done so.

The initial plan to house all the New Earth Song members was to build an additional three new homes to accompany the existing house. Unfortunately, the county informed us that the building code only permitted one duplex for that lot. This required them to rethink the housing model and inspired a new plan that entailed building one duplex with two large, shared living units. Within each living unit there would be designated individual space and shared accommodations for three families or a maximum of eight people, each containing a primary kitchen along with three wet bars. Another creative strategy involved reusing the top level of the existing home as an accessory building set adjacent to the new duplex that will house four offices, a guest room and common laundry facility. This shared housing model, echoing the earlier shared living experiences of Songaia, emerged as an alternative solution to the county code constraints.

Not Giving Up

Almost two years into the forming of New Earth Song, my husband, Phil, and I were looking at the first realistic cost estimates to build at

Alpaca Place, adjacent to Songaia. This was late in 2008, after the economic downturn had shredded the resources we were planning to use for our buy-in.

We honestly didn't see how we were going to come up with the funds, and had shared our dismay with the other New Earth Song members. My heart was broken and my stomach held a heaviness that wouldn't lift.

A few days later we received an email from Scotty and Patrick and Marlin (affectionately known as the Puppydogs) entitled "Love and Support from the Puppydogs." It told us how much we were loved and treasured, and included some brainstorming about alternative financial ideas: "Regardless of eventual details, PLEASE KNOW that there are many people (like me... and all of the Puppydogs) who love you a great deal...and who are now stretching to "think outside the box"—so that one day we can enjoy the pleasure of walking over to your home right next door."

That email told us we were enfolded in a community that wasn't going to give up on us. In the fall of 2009 we felt confident enough to commit our funds and now, in early 2010, we expect to build later this very year.

—Helen Gabel

Developing an Eco-neighborhood

The purchase of Alpaca Place and its subsequent transfer to the New Earth Song Community shaped an emerging long-range vision of an eco-neighborhood. This would include the addition of other community clusters interconnected in ways that would encourage sharing of resources and establishing an infrastructure that could help us reduce our carbon footprint. We realized that we could purchase adjacent properties as they became available, specifically on land south of us that had not already been consumed by developers.

In 2010 the property south of us became available again with better conditions for negotiating a reasonable selling price. The property was purchased by a group of five families from Songaia as a way to expand the community and as a step toward the realization of the eco-neighborhood. The image for this property was to reconfigure the existing large house into a shared living arrangement. Some of the investing members envision this house as a rental unit for Songaia associates, while others see the option of moving there as they age and/or desire to downsize.

The purchase of the south property resulted in various re-configurations. It was decided that Susie, from Alpaca Place, would purchase unit six from Jean, who would purchase unit two from Craig and Karly, who would move into the South property residence as renters. Chuck and Marilyn of Unit 13 decided to move into the South property as renters and rent out their unit. These moves shifted Susie's status from associate to owner member and Craig and Karly's status from owner member to associate members, while Chuck and Marilyn remained owner members of Songaia.

We are in an experimental stage of growing the community that includes an expansion of Songaia associates at the same time that we are creating smaller community groups within the larger community. There is both formal and informal aspects to these community relationships. The formal configurations are necessary to facilitate the legal/financial responsibilities of Songaia Cohousing Association, while for most everything else we consider ourselves full participants in the Songaia community.

CHAPTER TEN

What We Have Learned

Learning how to live in community is like learning to be a parent. There are skills that can be developed in preparation and observations that provide insights about how to live in community, but there is a learning process that only takes place while actually living in community.

Asking the Appropriate Questions

One of the most transformative learning experiences occurred in setting up our food program. Some of the community members who were part of the early stages of formation had experienced a cooperative meal program based on a flat monthly fee. They proposed a similar fee structure for the full community after the 2000 move-in. There were many concerns about whether everyone should be paying the same amount if we weren't all eating the same number of meals. After much discussion it was proposed and accepted that we try a three-month experiment where everyone paid the same regardless of how many meals they ate.

Throughout the three-month experiment, the positive attributes became clear and overshadowed the concerns about fairness. We realized that the question that we needed to ask was, "Are you getting enough for what you're paying?" as opposed to "Is this equitable?" Another way to ask this question is, "Are your food needs being met, if not, what more do you need?"

This shift in emphasis from "getting my fair share" to "are my needs being met?" allowed us to look at other community practices with a fresh perspective. It helped us to recognize the larger question of whether the community's needs are being met.

Expectations of Participation

Another transformative learning that we realized over time was how the distribution of community work was going to be accomplished. For example, many expected that in the planning stages we would all do our fair share and the workload would be distributed evenly. It soon became clear that various members were not in a position, or were not willing to do as much as others, either because of the need to care for their children, their professional involvement, or their unavailability for a variety of reasons. One early response was an attempt to require all residents to put so many hours in the garden. Not only was this unsuccessful, it often required more energy than it was worth to try and hold members accountable. This realization helped shape our future expectations.

The work expectations became tempered over time. After moving in, there was a flurry of activity in which it seemed everyone was engaged. This did not last very long. As people settled into their own homes it became more difficult to pull together community work parties. There was a time of adjusting to new patterns of participation. Each member was deciding how they would participate in the various tasks and projects. It became clear people were choosing the types of projects that they would willingly do. We acknowledged this as a community and called this basis for the distribution of work the "passion principle," and it replaced the notion that everyone would do equal work, which we realized was unrealistic and an unhelpful expectation.

The challenge then was how to identify and release each member's passion in a way that it benefited the whole community. What has emerged is a variety of activities and projects that reflect the diversity within the community.

Documenting Our Learnings

"Cohousing: What have we learned?" was the focus question in a 2005 Songaia Sharing Circle. Interestingly, the notion of a common "we" was perceived as an anomaly. There was some resistance to the notion that we could speak with a common voice. However, with a little persuasion, we embarked on a two-hour adventure in cooperative writing. What follows is the product of this cooperative process.

Learning: *Community living requires setting personal boundaries*
Life in community is a balancing act! Your priorities are always in play with those of other community members. Living closely requires one to continually evolve a personal matrix of relationships, remembering other's needs, preferences, strengths and foibles. A successful communitarian learns to care for his/her self by developing good boundaries of commitment, time and empathy. Deep connections come through patient daily interactions as well as in response to special or emergency situations.

Learning: *Flexibility helps*
One of the challenges and joys of community life is learning about flexibility.

When individuals have formed strongly held beliefs, before a decision has been processed by the group, they may be in conflict with forming an authentic consensus. There is sometimes a need to postpone personal agendas/schemes to support the group's needs.

A "dark side" of flexibility may be apathy. Being "flexible" about decisions in order to avoid conflict may be appropriate on occasion, but has risks of fostering alienation on a continuous basis.

Learning: *Setting guidelines around children is challenging*
We have individual family styles and values around child rearing, and it is important to us to maintain family autonomy. It takes deliberate and focused effort. At the same time we enjoy building relationships with all the community adults and children through mentoring, sharing childcare, enjoying community activities and shared work. The children interact with each other independently, developing something like extended-family relationships with each other as well as with adults outside their own family. Even so, there are few community agreements around parenting.

Learning: *Sharing and honoring different perspectives works*
Don't assume people have the same basic assumptions as you. Community provides the opportunity to experience these differences. By staying in relationship you learn to value and appreciate other points of view. Provide time to explicitly share what your assumptions are, like in sharing circles.

We are a conglomerate of individuals who share both similarities and differences. We have learned to recognize and honor defining elements that preserve our uniqueness, while acknowledging and nurturing the cohesive elements that bring us together.

Learning: *Sifting/pre-sorting helps in making community decisions*
Sifting and pre-sorting decisions has been helpful in our community. In general we don't decide items in a full group meeting unless necessary. One tool we use to help decide when it is necessary is the decision board. The decision board allows us to identify "passionates" on a topic, discern when consensus is possible without a meeting, and provides feedback on a proposal in a clear, time-sensitive way.

We have a diversity of processors regarding decisions. Some need to see the large picture before deciding. Some folks need to pre-digest proposals more than others. Some people trust a sub-group to decide items. We also think it is important to recognize that e-mail processing of decisions is limited.

Learning: *The "passion principle" works*
Several years ago we encouraged each person to work in the garden for only two hours per week. It didn't work! We know we cannot mandate participation, only invite. As the years went by, we noticed that those who contributed time and energy in a particular arena were often those who had a passion for the task or outcome. We now talk about our mode of participation as utilizing the "passion principle."

Learning: *Synergy happens in community*
The economic aspects include shared access to high-speed internet, resulting in community members paying only 10% of what it would cost individually. Bulk buying of food is benefiting us by providing a wide variety of items at a greatly reduced cost. Sharing of tools and skills allows for projects and repairs to be done at a very low cost.

People of diverse backgrounds and skills working together make results possible that otherwise would not be tackled. We experienced this in re-positioning concrete slabs to create a new walkway to the Common House. It took a team of about six men with 6-10' pry bars plus a tractor with a front-end loader to move 4'x4' and 4'x6' slabs, the larger of which the tractor could not even lift off the ground.

Doing things together, like watching movies, gets people related.

Learning: *Integrating is part of becoming a community*
This occurs in many ways, including singing, which builds community feelings, where extended family members become a part

of the community's life, and when there is a sense of pride in where you live—I'm a Songaian...

It also involves welcoming new members into the community, which is no easy task. How do you inculcate the "feel" of Songaia that people refer to with admiration?

Learning: *This experiment of living together is messy*

How does one decide what to do when the harmony of the community is disturbed? None of us likes conflict, we tend to defer and delay and only intervene when the level of discomfort becomes high. Resolution is frequently achieved only when a small group decides to act on behalf of the community's well-being to facilitate a resolution. The successful communitarian chooses to engage in spite of uncertainty of outcome.

Learning: *"Getting enough" is more important than "equality"*

Eating, cooking, and cleaning together five meals a week is a primary point of contact for everyone in our community. It is where we really get to know each other, our changing needs as well as our current mood and status. It is where we discover that some people don't like kale and learn to adapt a flexible approach to menu planning and food preparation. It is also where we learn how to meet a range of needs, but what may be most important, the food program is where we learn a basic principle in community living, that the question is not whether everyone is cared for equally, but, rather, is everyone receiving enough.

Five years later, in early 2010, we held another Sharing Circle and reflected on what we have learned over the last ten years. We may be five years older, the children have grown older and we have experienced the death of Stan, a community member, and the addition of associate members, but what we confirmed is that these "learnings" still hold true. Along with these demographic changes has come the awareness of greater flexibility and acceptance of each other, and we have learned to make a greater effort of working out our differences and being gentle with each other.

Ultimately, in living together, we have discovered what really matters is learning to trust each other. Community relies on trusting relationships to thrive and these "learnings" are what have worked for us in building that trust.

The Dream Continues to Unfold

E ven as this book was being completed the community was experiencing the dramatic deaths of two of its founding members. The profound loss of two highly engaged elders in the course of a year had a significant impact on each individual and left major holes in the community's fabric. It set in motion a time of fundamental transition, requiring members to step into new leadership roles as well as rethink the practical flow of everyday tasks. It also triggered much shared reflection and an opening for renewal and newness. The publication of this book has given us the opportunity to look back at this unfolding process and see that out of our sense of loss has emerged new community patterns, a determined spirit of inventiveness and an embracing of Fred and Stan's vision to "carry on."

Songaia's two departed founders were highly engaged community leaders. They were do-ers: organizing and leading community events, cooking regularly, active in the garden, framing ideas, and each had frequent interactions with many members of the community. Perhaps most profound for some was the loss of two mentors; these men were elders who blessed us with their deep listening and authentic presence.

Broken Threads Are
Taken Up by Many Hands

As they left us, some of the broken threads were grasped by others. Some holes simply had to be filled to continue our well-established patterns. For example, our food program requires five lead cooks per week. Without Stan and Fred, both of whom embraced the lead role, other people were called to lead more often and some new people began to cook. Both men provided the community with superb facilitation skills, and their absence creates opportunities for others. We are witnessing the growth of other adults as they assume these vital roles.

Creating Neighborhood

Never having met Stan, a new family joined us in early 2011. Michael has provided leadership by interviewing community members to pull together our visions about the future. Brent, another member, has facilitated a series of meetings and workshops using the methods once taught by Fred and Stan. Most of the community members—both residents of the Songaia property and owners of adjoining properties—are meeting to build a comprehensive vision and strategic plan for establishing a new, larger neighborhood consisting of multiple properties, including Songaia, New Earth Song and Life Song Commons. This neighborhood may be expanded to include other adjoining properties in the coming years.

What lies ahead for Songaia and its growing number of associates? We don't know. We do have many creative ideas, some of which will become reality. We anticipate new patterns as our dreams continue to unfold.

Remarkable Farewells

The night before Stan passed away, he participated in a community circle that looked back at the community's 20-year history and kicked off our visioning for the next decade. With another member, he closed the circle with a reflection on the circle itself. In those precious moments, Stan named our first decade as "Inventing," our second as "Growing," and suggested that our next decade might be "Re-inventing." This forward-looking message has been embraced by the community as we re-envision our small cohousing community as part of a larger community neighborhood.

On Fred's last night, September 9, 2010, community members gathered around him as he struggled for breath. Each of us had a few moments to speak with him individually and then we sang some of his favorite songs as he joined in. Unlike Stan's death, which came quickly and without warning, Fred's last hours were the closing verses of a three-year journey to dying. His final words to one of our members was "Carry On."

Stan Crow and Fred Lanphear

Made in the USA
Coppell, TX
11 March 2021